D0983173

THE CONSEQUENCES OF
DECISION-MAKING

The Consequences of Decision-Making

NILS BRUNSSON

OXFORD
UNIVERSITY PRESS

OXFORD
UNIVERSITY PRESS

Great Clarendon Street, Oxford OX2 6DP

Oxford University Press is a department of the University of Oxford.
It furthers the University's objective of excellence in research, scholarship,
and education by publishing worldwide in

Oxford New York

Auckland Cape Town Dar es Salaam Hong Kong Karachi
Kuala Lumpur Madrid Melbourne Mexico City Nairobi
New Delhi Shanghai Taipei Toronto

With offices in

Argentina Austria Brazil Chile Czech Republic France Greece
Guatemala Hungary Italy Japan Poland Portugal Singapore
South Korea Switzerland Thailand Turkey Ukraine Vietnam

Oxford is a registered trade mark of Oxford University Press
in the UK and in certain other countries

Published in the United States
by Oxford University Press Inc., New York

British Library Cataloguing in Publication Data
Data available

Library of Congress Cataloging in Publication Data
Data available

Typeset by SPi Publisher Services, Pondicherry, India
Printed in Great Britain
on acid-free paper by
Biddles Ltd., King's Lynn, Norfolk

ISBN 978–0–19–920628–5

1 3 5 7 9 10 8 6 4 2

Jacket illustration: © Oscar Reutersvärd/BUS 2006

Contents

Preface

This book contains a collection of articles on a common theme: the role of decisions in organizations. The articles have been published elsewhere, and I have not changed any of them, however tempted I have sometimes been. The articles reflect a continuous discussion of a limited number of ideas over a long period. Yet, there is much more to do. I hope that the ideas presented here can stimulate further theorizing about the causes and consequences of decisions.

Nils Brunsson
Ingeby, September 2006

Acknowledgements

We are grateful for permission to reproduce the following material in this volume:

Reprinted from *Accounting, Organizations, and Society*, vol. 15, Nils Brunsson, 'Deciding for Responsibility and Legitimation: Alternative Interpretations of Organizational Decision-Making', pages 47–58, © 1990, with permission from Elsevier.

'The Irrationality of Action and Action Rationality: Decisions, Ideologies, and Organizational Actions', by Nils Brunsson, reprinted from the *Journal of Management Studies*, Blackwell Publishing.

'Implementing Reforms', by Nils Brunsson and Hans Winberg, reprinted from *The Reforming Organization*, edited by Nils Brunsson and J. P. Olsen, Fagbokforlaget, 1997.

'Responsibility as an Impediment to Influence: The Case of Budgeting', reprinted from *The Organization of Hypocrisy: Talk, Decisions, and Actions in Organizations* by Nils Brunsson, Liber, 1989.

'Industrial Policy as Implementation or Legitimation' by Nils Brunsson, reprinted from *Organizing Industrial Development*, edited by R. Wolff, de Gruyter, 1986.

'Organized Hypocrisy' by Nils Brunsson, reprinted from *The Northern Lights*, edited by B. Czarniawsk and G. Sévon, Liber, 2003.

Reprinted from *Sociology of Organizations*, vol. 13, Nils Brunsson, 'Ideas and Actions: Justification and Hypocrisy as Alternatives to Control', pages 211–35, © 1995, with permission from Elsevier.

1

Decision as Institution

Decision is usually understood to be synonymous with choice, whether we are speaking of life in general or of academic theories. In this book, I argue that it is more fruitful to treat decision as an institution—as a well-known pattern of action with a ready-made account and with rules that are taken for granted (Jepperson 1991). People, particularly in organizations, are often involved in a process called decision-making. We take for granted that some people in some situations make decisions and what this decision-making involves: to consider what is desirable, to contemplate possible actions, and to choose one of them. This is a common pattern of behaviour. Some organizations or parts of organizations, such as parliaments, boards, or management teams, are expected to make many decisions; and decision-making is expected to be their main activity. The media devote a considerable portion of their reports to describing decisions. The ready-made account or rationale for decisions is the idea that they serve the purpose of choice.

There are rules for making decisions—rules that we take for granted. In some cases the rule is to follow rules; we consider it appropriate to use a rule-following form of intelligence. A court is expected to make decisions according to the rules of law, for example; it is expected to consider which law is most appropriate in each particular case. However, in most cases we expect another form of intelligence: that of intentionality. Our intentions—what we want to achieve in the future—shall guide our decisions. And we are more and more often expected to try to achieve our intentions in the most effective and efficient way—to be rational. According to the rule of rationality, we ought to make decisions by clarifying our preferences, examining all our action options and all the consequences of these options, and then compare preferences with consequences in order to find, and subsequently adopt, the option offering the best consequences for our preferences.

The rule of rationality is highly celebrated in modern societies. Decisions are often criticized on the grounds that the underlying decision process has not been rational enough. A lack of rationality is generally seen to be a problem.

As a practice, however, decision processes have several causes and consequences other than choice, which is one reason why they tend not to be rational. Decision processes are social phenomena, and as such they need to

be investigated in their own right, without prejudice—without the precon-
ception that they are always and merely processes of choice. Choice is another
important phenomenon deserving of study, but we should not confuse it with
decision. The theme of this book is the consequences of decisions.

DECISION, THE INDIVIDUAL, AND THE ORGANIZATION

It is not by chance that the institution of decision and the rule of rationality
are important. They are closely connected to another fundamental institution
that has a strong and pervasive presence in modern society: the individual
(Meyer 1986; Gergen 1991). We tend to assume that we are individuals and
that all other humans are individuals as well. We ought to be individuals; we
often attempt to behave as individuals; and there is a moral and legal system
of rules based upon the supposition that we are individuals.

The individual comprises a system of rules creating a pattern of action
that is taken for granted. To see human beings as individuals involves the
assumption that they are actors—entities with clear boundaries, possessing
sovereignty and autonomous or self-interested goals and rational means
(Meyer et al. 1987). The individual is assumed to have a strong identity.
The individual is a composite, an 'indivisible' whole with clear boundaries.
The individual is presumed to have special characteristics that are relatively
stable in time and space. The individual also has free will—the ability to
choose thoughts and wishes freely. The institution of the individual encompasses an assumption of hierarchy—a hierarchy of thought and deed. As
individuals, our actions are expected to be controlled by our thoughts, and our
identity to be realized in our actions. The assumption that individuals choose
and control their own actions and have a free will makes them responsible for
their actions.

Individuals are expected to make choices. The institution of decision
reflects the basic notion of individuals as autonomous actors, free to choose
their actions and their futures according to their own specific identities. When
individuality is an important value, we can expect people to present many
decisions and to think of their actions as being preceded by decisions.

The form of intelligence that best fits this view is intentionality; we are supposed to choose actions that allow us to achieve our intentions in the future.
The most appropriate logic for realizing this aim is rationality (Brunsson 2006:
ch. 1). In this case, the analysis starts from something that is the individual's
own: intentions and preferences. Intentions and preferences are a means of
describing identity. A rational analysis is a subsequent attempt to secure the
hierarchy, ensuring that preferences and actions correspond and that the

preferences truly control the actions. If we can prove that we are rational, we simultaneously demonstrate that we are proper individuals.

Forms of intelligence other than intentionality and rationality fail to create a good fit with the institution of the individual. Following the rules of others or imitating others may be common and perfectly sensible ways of acting, but they are difficult to combine with the presentation of oneself as a full-fledged or 'true' individual. They imply that it is the rules or conduct of others that are central, not something that belongs to the individual.

In a society of individuals, we can expect rationality to be a form of intelligence that is accorded high status. In our society, both the theory of the individual and rationality as a form of intelligence are almost always given the status of clearly correct and respectable phenomena; they are parts of the institutionalized reality. People are called individuals, and rationality is seen as being equivalent to intelligence, or at least as being the only proper intelligence. In a secularized culture, it seems more appropriate that the future is controlled by the choices of human beings rather than by God, fate, or chance.

The Organization as Individual

The basic features of the individual as a mental image are found in another central institution: the formal organization. Like human beings, organizations are often perceived as being a type of individual (Brunsson 1997). They are even 'legal persons' under the law. Organizations are perceived as having a clear identity; they have clear boundaries, special characteristics, and special tasks or business concepts. Organizations are also perceived as incorporating some form of hierarchy; they have an authoritative centre—management— that controls and coordinates their actions. Management ensures that the organization's task or the business concept is transformed into action. Organizations have a certain degree of independence, and management has a certain freedom of choice.

The fact that an organization is envisaged as a type of individual makes intentionality and rationality the forms of intelligence best suited for the organization in general. Even though those who work on lower rungs of the organizational ladder must follow the rules set by management, the organization as a whole is expected to be intentional and rational. Top management should make rational decisions. The organization's identity is frequently described in terms of goals—specifications of the future state it will attain. It is also easy to reconcile rationality with ideas about effectiveness and efficiency; rational decisions are decisions that lead to the actions that most effectively and most efficiently lead to the desired result. Effectiveness and efficiency are central requirements in organizations.

THEORIES OF DECISION

Strong modern institutions tend to have a strong scientific backing (Drori et al. 2003). The institution of decison is supported by social science theories that describe almost all human actions as the result of decisions. Such theories are common in the field of economics. Sometimes it is even assumed that decisions are basically rational and that we can deduce people's preferences by observing their behaviour (Samuelson 1947: ch. 5).

When it comes to research on decision-making processes, the beliefs and norms of the decision institution have set much of the research agenda. Scholars have shared the general, institutional assumption that decisions in themselves are intentional acts, and that the intention behind decisions is to choose among future action options. The terms 'decision' and 'choice' have generally been treated as identical concepts. Both the cause and the effects of decisions are assumed to involve choice: decision-makers make decisions in order to make choices, and the essential result of decisions is choice.

Scholars have also assumed that decision-makers are striving, or should be striving, to achieve a high degree of rationality. Rationality is a demanding form of intelligence, and studies of decisions have revealed that people are often systematically irrational in their decision-making processes. The rule of rationality is not strong when it comes to controlling people's behaviour. Instead of examining many options and their consequences, we often examine few—sometimes only one (Lindblom 1959). We base our decisions on our present preferences, even though we realize they may change (March 1978). We assess consequences by rules of thumb, which are often highly misleading (Nisbett and Ross 1980). Or we fail to act according to the decisions we have made (Brunsson 2002). Deviations from the rational model are regularly discussed as failures that demand explanation.

A vast body of literature has emerged, the task of which is to help decision-makers improve the rationality of their behaviour—the standard theme of normative management literature. Most management fashions, such as management by objectives, quality programmes, balanced scorecards, or business process re-engineering are, to a great extent, programmes for increased rationality. The manager must have clear goals; these goals must be communicated in a clear way; and these goals will then control organizational actions.

By reading business school course materials, in fact, it is easy to obtain the impression that 'management' equals 'rational decision-making'.

Theories Inside and Outside Institutions

One can say that many decision theories have been based on a perspective 'from within' the institution of decision. Like other people in our culture, scholars have taken basic aspects of the institution for granted. Research from within institutions seems generally sensible and useful because it treats what we perceive as important issues and promises to solve what we believe to be important problems. But it also reinforces our institutions.

An alternative slant is to examine institutions 'from the outside'. This type of research is likely to ask a different set of questions. Why do certain types of actors emerge at all? Why do they pursue their particular interests and intentions? Why do they perceive certain problems, and why do they try to solve them in a certain way? Instead of taking institutionalized conceptions for granted, scholars in this mould ask why certain things are taken for granted and what effects may arise when we assume this position. A perspective from the outside is critical rather than useful.

In this book, the research agenda is triggered more by a perspective from outside the decision institution than from inside. In the chapters to follow, it is not taken for granted that the cause and consequence of decisions is choice of actions. It is not even assumed that there is always necessarily a relationship between decision and action. We can expect to see decisions without actions and actions without decisions. Nor is it taken for granted that decision-makers strive for a high degree of rationality—much less that they achieve it. Instead I discuss possible consequences of decisions beyond choice. And what is the effect on decision-makers and decision processes of the assumption that decisions lead to choices? What circumstances evoke a strong demand for rationality in decision processes, and under what circumstances are such demands less prominent? When do decision-makers strive towards rationality, and when do they seek to design their decision process according to some other tenet? What are the causes and effects of rationality and irrationality in decision processes? Is it even wise to be rational?

In much of decision theory, the existence of decision-makers and decision-making is taken for granted, but the answers to the questions in the previous paragraph may also help us to understand why there are decision-makers and decisions at all. On the basis of the analysis in the book we can discuss such questions as what motivates people to make decisions, when or in what situations decisions are made and when they are not, and what actions are and are not preceded by decisions.

Consequences of Decision-Making

The causes and consequences of decisions do not necessarily correspond. Decision-making commonly occurs because there is an institutional rule saying that decisions must be made. The consequences of decision processes and decisions are manifold. In this book I discuss three consequences other than choice: the mobilization of action, responsibility, and legitimacy. Decisions can support or undermine action, and the way in which decisions are made influences the chances of mobilizing action. Decisions are powerful instruments for creating responsibility; by presenting actions, events, or situations as results of decisions, decision-makers dramatize their own importance and influence and, therefore, their responsibility. By accepting responsibility, decision-makers transfer their own legitimacy to actions, events, and situations. In other cases, decisions can create legitimacy by compensating for actions in another direction. Decisions sometimes lead to choices of action and actions are sometimes chosen in ways other than by decisions.

When decision-makers are aware of all possible consequences of their decisions, they may actively try to use decision processes for supporting or reducing some of the consequences. So the consequences may become part of the decision-makers' purposes and thereby become partial causes of decisions and characteristics of the decision-making process. All in all, decision processes tend to become much more complex than they would have been, had the only effect and purpose been choice.

If decisions have consequences other than choice, it is not obvious that it is wise to try to follow the institutionalized rules of rationality. Decision-makers with purposes other than choice may want to break these rules. But such attempts are difficult to justify in a world where decisions are defined as choice and the merits of rationality are taken for granted.

THE CONSEQUENCES OF DECISION

The next chapter provides an overview of the four consequences of decisions: choice, action, responsibility, and legitimacy. Several of the empirical studies described in the other chapters are referred to in Chapter 2, and the effects of various consequences on the decision processes are addressed. Different consequences imply different decision process designs, information usage, costs, and needs for making decisions at all. The degree of rationality in decision processes tends to vary according to the consequences foreseen by the decision-makers. High degrees of rationality can be interpreted as attempts to prevent action, evade responsibility, or support organizational legitimacy in a conflicting environment.

Mobilizing Action

Chapters 3 to 7 contain in-depth discussions of each of the four consequences. In Chapter 3, I address the effect of decisions on organizational action. The main argument is that decision-makers who choose to or must stick closely to the rule of rationality may be likely to make good choices; but they are also likely to face difficulties in realizing their decisions. Mobilizing organizational actions is easier when decision processes are systematically irrational— when decision-makers consider only one action option for instance, and when preferences and consequences that support this alternative are the only ones considered.

This relationship between decision and action is dependent upon the tendency of decisions to produce both certainty and uncertainty. The institutionalized purpose of decisions is to achieve certainty, to determine and stabilize the future. But because decisions are interpreted as choices, they also produce uncertainty by highlighting the fact that the choice could have been different (Luhmann 2000: ch. 4)—or perhaps *should* have been different (Festinger 1957; Harrison and March 1984)—and that the future is dependent upon the whims of human beings rather than upon stable, reliable entities. Moreover, attempts at rationality in decision processes tend to dramatize any potential uncertainty that exists in a situation.

An alternative is to employ a rule-following logic. The rules may have been produced by what, in Chapter 3, is called 'organizational ideology': shared ideas about the organization's situation and about appropriate actions in the organization. If such an ideology is clear and precise and is shared by all the decision-makers—if it represents a strong local institution—it can, to a considerable extent, dictate the choice of action. Because the choice has already been made, any decision processes that are undertaken have other effects and can be used for other purposes. They can be used for mobilizing action, for instance; as choice is not the purpose or effect of the decision, it is easier to avoid rationality and employ systematic irrationality.

These observations parallel earlier observations in the social sciences about the coordinating effects of institutions on a societal level. Institutions that represent clear and widely shared ideas and rules facilitate coordination and collective action in societies (Berger and Luckmann 1966). If people's behaviour were guided primarily by individual rationality rather than by common rules, it would become more difficult to mobilize coordination and collective action, and such action would occur only under certain, specific circumstances (Olson 1965).

The recognition that rationality and action are difficult to combine has sometimes been used as an argument for rationality. The flag of rationality was raised by many people who wanted to prevent a repetition of the highly effective but evil organizational actions that were achieved by some states in the middle of the twentieth century. And rationality is also often advocated in more mundane circumstances by people who want to stop specific actions. A classic trick among oppositional groups is to try to obstruct or delay actions by attempting to increase rationality in decision processes by arguing that more preferences, alternatives, and consequences should be analysed and taken into account.

But when action is both vital and difficult to achieve—as it is in many large organizations—rationality is less wise. From the discussion in Chapter 3, it can be concluded that rationality is not likely to be the most intelligent mode for making the 'big' decisions involving complex, coordinated actions with serious long-term and uncertain consequences, but it may be the best choice for the 'small' decisions involving simple actions with primarily short-term effects. Action is facilitated by a specific type of intelligence described in the chapter as 'action rationality'. Action rationality proves to be a combination of rule-following and systematic irrationality, and a more relevant term might be 'action intelligence'.

Implementation and 'Determination'

In Chapter 4, I continue to analyse the relationship between decision and action, using a case study to illustrate the classical problem of decision implementation. Many discussions of decision-making build on the assumption that decisions concern actions that are easily compared with the decision and try to determine if the two correspond. But many of the most elaborate and time-consuming decision processes in organizations concern decisions that are at least one step away from action—decisions about policies, principles, or oganizational forms, for example. The decision used as an illustration in Chapter 4 concerns an organizational reform.

One implementation problem is the relationship between the simplicity of decisions and the complexity of action. It is easy to gain support for decisions on simple principles, but such principles tend not to provide much guidance for action. Another implementation problem is time. Most models of organizational control and decision implementation are build on the idea that decision-makers are slow and actors are quick. Decisions are supposed to be stable, at least as long as it takes to implement the corresponding action. In Chapter 4, I discuss what can happen when this is not the case: when decisions change more quickly than action.

Not only do decision-makers who want to influence actions have an implementation problem, they also have what could be called a determination problem: a problem controlling the contents of their own decisions. In order to learn what action they want and in order to secure some chance of implementation, they must often interact with prospective implementers who have valuable information. But such interaction sometimes leads to the implementers' strongly influencing the choice (Brunsson 2002: ch. 4). In Chapter 5, I illustrate how this problem can be further complicated by the responsibility consequence of decisions by using the example of budget processes. The analysis of the relationship between the choice and responsibility consequences of decisions demonstrates that responsibility may undermine choice. Having the position of responsible decision-maker may obstruct rather than promote one's influence on the contents of decisions.

Responsibility and Hypocrisy

In Chapter 6, I discuss the relationship between responsibility and legitimacy. The analysis is illustrated with the case of a top-level government decision, demonstrating how the responsibility effect of decisions can be used in attempts at creating legitimacy for a situation rather than for an action. Decisions may create legitimacy for decision-makers and for social situations, even when they are not implemented and even when they have no positive practical effects. To create this type of legitimacy is an important task for politicians in modern societies who are often delegated the unsolvable problems of their societies.

In other situations, legitimacy for organizations, decision-makers, and actions can be enhanced by decisions that contradict actions. The theme of Chapter 7 is hypocrisy—the inverted relationship between decision and action. Hypocrisy is a response to a world in which values, ideas, or people are in conflict—a way in which individuals and organizations handle such conflicts. It is a way of trying to satisfy some demands by talk or decisions and others by action. Situations of conflicting demands often make it easier to act in one direction if the decision indicates the opposite: the more clear is the decision that is made about an action, the lower the likelihood that that action will actually be taken. The probability of an action increases if what is decided is in opposition to it. Decisions in one direction compensate for actions in the opposite direction and vice versa.

In order to choose or mobilize actions, decisions must be made before actions. In order to establish responsibility and create legitimacy, however, this is not always necessary; instead it is often wise to make decisons after the actions—when there is no uncertainty about which action has been taken.

The responsibility and hypocrisy consequences of decisons are dependent upon the institutionalized concept of decision as choice and upon theories supporting this conception. Because decison-makers are seen to have chosen an action, they become responsible for it. And hypocrisy works only if people interested in a certain action pay attention to decisions, even if they have not been realized in action. A reason they have for doing so is provided by traditional decision theories based on the assumption that decisions increase the likelihood of the corresponding action being implemented.

The responsibility consequence arises even if people are aware of it. Hypocrisy, on the other hand, tends not to work when people are aware. If people believe in hypocrisy—if they believe that a decision in one direction decreases the likelihood of action in the same direction—they will not put a positive value on a decision that corresponds to the actions they want. Decison-makers who want to accept responsibility or want their hypocrisy to work must support the belief that decisons are about choice, thus reproducing and reinforcing the institution of decison.

Talk and Action

In the last chapter of the book, I discuss the relationship between ideas and actions. Decisions can be described as a kind of talk. In the last chapter I address a further standard assumption of the relationship between decisons and actions—namely the assumption that what can be said can be done and what can be done can be said. This conjecture is not always true, which makes it impossible to achieve consistency between decision and action. In such situations, decisions tend to become hypocritical. Furthermore, decisons belong more to the world of ideas than to the world of action. These worlds have different characteristics, and their differences are often an important factor behind the decision-makers' difficulty in controlling actions. Problems of control tend to turn decisions into justifications rather than causes of actions. By discussing the relationships among talk, ideas, and actions, the chapter also summarizes some central arguments in the preceding chapters.

In sum, the arguments in this book give a more complex picture of decision-making than most traditional decision theories do. Politicians, managers, and other organizational leaders play important roles as decision-makers, but their roles are much more complex than implied by the notion of decisions as mere choices. Management is not only about choosing the right action. To a great extent, it is about making many other choices: choosing the issues to decide about and choosing when to abstain from decisions, for instance; choosing to make decisions consistent or inconsistent with actions; or choosing to make decisions before or after actions. And different decison-makers in the same decison processes may strive for different options; thus the process itself may deal with which will dominate as much as it deals with the choice of action. All this is what makes management a complex and fascinating art rather than a simple technique.

The chapters consist of articles or book chapters that have been written and published over the past twenty years. Not surprisingly, therefore, the terminology is somewhat inconsistent, and the chapters relate, in part, to somewhat different scientific debates. And it has not been possible to avoid a certain degree of repetition. Rather than providing one straight line of argument, the chapters provide variations on a common theme. I hope that these variations together form more of a symphony than a cacophony, and that the reader will tolerate some repetition of the general arguments in order to arrive at the more detailed elaborations in each chapter. I also hope that this book can stimulate further research on the intricacies of decisions and decision-making. It is a field that is far more complex and more fascinating than its institutionalized conceptions might lead us to believe.

REFERENCES

Berger, P. L. and Luckmann, T. (1966). *The Social Construction of Reality*. Garden City, NY: Doubleday.

Brunsson, N. (1997). 'Organizational Individuality and Rationality as Reform Content', in N. Brunsson and J. P. Olsen (eds.), *The Reforming Organization*, 2nd edn. Bergen, Norway: Fagbokforlaget. First edition published by Routledge 1993.

_____ (2002). *The Organization of Hypocrisy. Talk, Decisions and Actions in Organizations*, 2nd edn. First edition published by Wiley 1989.

_____ (2006). *Mechanisms of Hope. Maintaining the Dream of Rationality in Organizations*. Malmö: Liber Copenhagen Business Press.

Drori, G. S., Meyer, J. W., Ramirez, F. O., and Schofer, E. (2003). *Science in the Modern World Polity. Institutionalization and Globalization*. Stanford, CA: Stanford University Press.

Festinger, L. (1957). *A Theory of Cognitive Dissonance*. Stanford, CA: Stanford University Press.

Gergen, K. J. (1991). *The Saturated Self. Dilemmas of Identity in Contemporary Life*. Basic Books.

Harrison, J. R. and March, J. G. (1984). 'Decision-Making and Postdecision Surprises', *Administrative Science Quarterly*, 29: 26–42.

Jepperson, R. L. (1991). 'Institutions, Institutional Effects, and Institutionalism', in W. W. Powell and P. J. DiMaggio (eds.), *The New Institutionalism in Organizational Analysis*. Chicago, IL: University of Chicago Press.

Lindblom, C. E. (1959). 'The Science of "Muddling-Through" ', *Public Administration Review*, 19: 79–88.

Luhmann, N. (2000). *Organisation und Entscheidung*. Opladen, Germany: Westdeutscher Verlag.

March, J. G. (1978). 'Bounded Rationality, Ambiguity, and the Engineering of Choice', *Bell Journal of Economics*, 9(2): 587–608.

Meyer, J. W. (1986). 'Myths of Socialization and of Personality', in Thomas C. Heller, Morton Sosna, and David E. Wellbery (eds.), *Reconstructing Individualism. Autonomy, Individuality, and the Self in Western Thought*. Stanford, CA: Stanford University Press.

—— Boli, J., and Thomas, G. M. (1987). 'Ontology and Rationalization in the Western Cultural Account', in George M. Thomas, John W. Meyer, Francisco O. Ramirez, and John Boli (eds.), *Institutional Structure. Constituting State, Society, and the Individual*. Beverly Hills, CA: Sage.

Nisbett, R. and Ross, L. (1980). *Human Inference*. Englewood Cliffs, NJ: Prentice-Hall.

Olson, M. (1965). *The Logic of Collective Action*. New York: Schocken.

Samuelson, P. (1947). *Foundations of Economic Analysis*. Cambridge, MA: Harvard University Press.

2

Deciding for Responsibility and Legitimation: Alternative Interpretations of Organizational Decision-Making

Decision-making has long been an important field for research on organizations. Perhaps as a partial result of this, decisions are also an important organizational activity: organizations often say that they make decisions and they sometimes behave roughly in accordance with what is described in decision theory: they look for alternative future actions, they predict consequences, they compare consequences with preferences and they designate one alternative as the one decided. The contents of decision theories tend to vary depending on whether they are prescriptive or descriptive—descriptive theories typically report less rationality in actual decision processes than what is recommended in prescriptive theories. However, standard decision theory, both prescriptive and descriptive, is based on a common assumption—that decision-making and decisions serve the purpose of choice. Decisions have been described as choices and organizational choice has been analysed by describing decisions. In the same tradition, accounting has been considered an important source of information for decision-makers whose sole purpose is to choose the best action among a set of alternatives.

Recent descriptive studies (Brunsson 1982, 1985) have questioned the empirical validity of the equating of decision and choice and pointed at another role that organizational decisions sometimes play—the role of mobilizing organizational action, a role that requires less rationality than choice. But choice and mobilization are not the only roles of decision-making and decisions in organizations. In this chapter it will be argued that two additional roles exist—decisions may allocate responsibility and legitimacy to decision-makers and organizations. Consideration will also be given to how the different roles can explain the design of decision processes, the use of information and the number of decisions in organizations.

One way of learning about the roles of decision-making is to study organizations or organizational subunits that have specialized in this activity. For some organizations, decision-making constitutes one of their most time-consuming and most important activities, and decisions one of their most important outputs. Such organizations can be named decision-oriented: examples can be found among parliaments, councils, governments, and boards. The discussion in this chapter is based on empirical studies of decision processes in such organizations: in local governments, national governments, and company boards. The eight decision processes studied were all long and complicated. They concerned city budgets, investments and disinvestments, and governmental programmes. At a first glance they all could be interpreted as dealing with choice—preferences, alternatives, and consequences were discussed and they led to the presentation of one alternative as the one chosen. Intense studies of the processes and the decision-makers' arguments led to other interpretations, however; the details of the decision processes revealed them as dealing with mobilization, responsibility allocation, and legitimation rather than or in addition to choice.

DECISIONS AS CHOICES OR MOBILIZERS

The standard assumption that the purpose and main result of decision-making is choice is composed of a series of minor assumptions. The decision-makers are assumed to search for the best action among several alternatives. Decision-making can be described as problem-solving where the problem is constituted by the existence of more than one action alternative. The basic uncertainty thus relates to the alternatives. Normative decision theory prescribes how this problem should be solved by following the rules of rational decision-making: by establishing a preference function, listing all possible alternatives, describing all relevant consequences, and comparing them with the preference function. In practice, the problem may be more difficult, since the decision-makers may be uncertain or lack information not only about which alternatives there are and about the consequences or the preferences. Some aspects of these complications are handled by normative theories, but not all, and this may be one reason why actual decision-makers do not always follow the norms of rationality. Most decision-makers lack capacity or competence for the complicated information processing that rational decision-making requires (March and Simon 1958; Huysmans 1970; Kahneman and Tversky 1973; Nisbett and Ross 1980). Alternatively, decision-makers, problems solutions, and choice opportunities may interact randomly, producing a certain randomness in choices of alternatives (Cohen, March, and Olsen 1972).

Such explanations of deviations from the rational norms imply that even if the deviations are common, they do not undermine the norms themselves.

If the purpose of the decision-making is to choose the best alternative, there is no reason for not trying to adhere to the rational norms, although it is not possible always to succeed. Deviations are not functional.

This is different from theories in which decisions are seen as ways of finding out the choice prerequisites rather than the other way round. Decisions may also forego the recognition of preferences or consequences; we may decide in order to find or develop our preferences (March 1976) and we may decide and implement the decision to find out what consequences are attached to one alternative. Therefore, instead of waiting for uncertainty to be dissolved before the decision, the decision can be used for dissolving uncertainty. But sometimes decisions may not be connected to choice or the choice pre-requisites at all.

Organizations have more problems than choice. Another fundamental organizational problem is to achieve coordinated, collective action. It has been argued that decision-making and decisions are sometimes used for solving that problem, and that this affects the design of the decision process (Brunsson 1982, 1985). In order to mobilize organizational action, it is important to secure commitment from presumed actors. Commitment links the actor to the action in advance, it is a kind of promise of personal support to an action; committed actors can be supposed to contribute to the organizational action. Decision-making may be used as a way of forming commitments, both directly and indirectly. Decision processes can be instruments for the participants to express their commitment to the action decided on. They can also be used to create motivations and expectations for an action, strong enough for making actors become willing to commit themselves to the action.

Decision processes oriented to commitment building deal with uncertainty as to actors rather than uncertainty as to alternatives. This has implications for the design of the decision process (Brunsson 1982). The formation of commitment is facilitated by decision processes that systematically do not fol-low the norms of rational decision-making. Decision processes that deal with few or just one alternative and a biased set of positive consequences for one alternative express the decision-makers' commitment to the action alternative considered. The limitation to one or a few alternatives and to a biased set of consequences is facilitated if preferences are adapted to the alternatives rather than the other way round. The last step in the decision process, the formal designation of one alternative, is also important for expressing the commit-ment of the participants. So the involvement of the actors in a decision process following norms of irrationality is one instrument of expressing commitment. Decision processes following the rational norms, where the decision-makers describe several alternatives and both pros and cons with each alternative, can easily be used for avoiding commitment to any one action alternative.

Irrational decision processes can also make presumptive actors willing to commit themselves regardless of whether they are involved in the decision process or not. It has been argued that their commitment is dependent on their motivation and expectations. If the actors believe that the action is a good one and if they expect it to be carried out by the organization they are more apt to commit themselves to the action than if motivations and expectations do not exist (Brunsson 1985). Strong motivations and expectations for a specific action are enhanced by irrational decision processes which glorify one action and clearly designate it as materializing.

Rational and irrational decision processes have different needs for information. The rational model is greedy for data. It deals with many action alternatives and many consequences. The task is to predict the effects of different alternatives on predetermined goals. When these goals are very abstract, such as the goals of profitability or return on investment, a large number of diverse factors have to be predicted, as prescriptive models for investment calculation demonstrate. It is easy to see that fine-grained accounting data describing past performance can be highly valuable for making such predictions in a realistic way.

Irrational decision processes use fewer alternatives and thus less data. Since objectives are adapted to alternatives and data and not vice versa, there is less need for extensive information search. The data used are systematically biased towards favouring the action one is going to undertake. So not only is there less need for all the data that can be found in the accounting system, but also the presentation of unbiased accounting data may threaten the process, driving it towards more rationality. If accouting data are used at all, they should be used in a biased way and simple measures should be preferred to more complicated ones (Swieringa and Weick 1987).

The rational process expresses a predictive attitude towards the future, while the irrational process is closer to planning than prediction, closer to the task of determining what shall happen than to the task of guessing what will happen. When results are planned, information about the past is less relevant than when the task is prediction—the very purpose of the plan may be to change the results. The degree of rationality is an important determinant of to what extent and how accounting data can be used. In the following sections consideration is given to how the degree of rationality varies not only with the roles of choice versus mobilization but also with other roles.

The interpretations of decisions as choices and mobilizers both give the decision-makers an attractive role. They are supposed to affect the decision and subsequent actions. But when these are realized, there is nothing left with the decision-maker. This is often too rosy a picture of the role of decision-makers in practice, as will be described in the next section.

DECISION-MAKING AS RESPONSIBILITY ALLOCATION

Uncertainty may not only be connected to alternatives and actors, it may also concern decision-makers. Decision processes are sometimes used for handling that uncertainty, for clearly pointing out who are the decision-makers. This is the case when the decision processes are used for allocating responsibility.

Responsibility is a concept with several connotations, all describing a perceived relation between human beings and actions (Edwards 1969; Spiro 1969). One connotation has to do with the attribution of causes. If a person is perceived as being the cause of an event, he or she is considered responsible for it. This definition of responsibility is fundamental in law where it is closely connected to the concept of culpa and guilt and used as a basis for discussions of punishment (Ross 1975; French 1984). The causal definition of responsibility is also important in moral philosophy and can be argued to be the basis of other connotations, such as that of duty or obligation (Helkama 1981). In both western law and western moral philosophy since Aristotle responsibility has been considered to be dependent on the existence of voluntariness—only a person who actually wants to pursue an action is causing it; if the actor is forced by other people or things or the actions are just by chance, he or she is not causing them and therefore is not considered to be responsible. The question of voluntariness was already viewed by Aristotle in terms of choice. Actions at least look like voluntary ones if 'at the time they are performed they are the result of a deliberate choice between alternatives' (Aristotle, Book III, ch. 1). Later it has been argued that the existence of free will and self-identity through time are additional requirements for responsibility, but the basic connection of voluntarity and choice to responsibility has been commonplace in philosophic discussions into our time (Edwards 1969).

Psychological experiments under the label of attribution theory demonstrate no dramatic differences between the basic rules of moral philosophers and the rules laypersons use for designating persons as causing actions (Kelley 1972). Researchers have identified causes with responsibility to the extent that most empirical studies have not differentiated between the attribution of causes and the attribution of responsibility. However, the results still indicate that laypersons have the same basic tendency as philosophers and legal experts to relate causes and responsibility (Fincham and Jaspars 1980). It seems safe to assume that causal attribution is an important condition for responsibility allocation in practice although it may not always be sufficient.

In classical administrative theory the connection between power or authority and responsibility was considered to be a strong one: 'wheresoever authority is exercised responsibility arises' (Fayol 1949). Authority at high hierarchical levels is a means for individuals at lower levels to reduce their responsibility for their actions (Barnard 1938: 170), and the authority of higher levels is accepted just because it gives rise to responsibility (Simon 1965: ch. 7).

To sum up, responsibility is given to individuals who are observed (by themselves or others) to have affected events (or just their own actions) by having freely chosen and carried out one of several possible actions or inactions. People hold others responsible if they believe that they have made decisions influencing events and if they think of these decisions as choices. But such beliefs are not necessarily shared—the influence on events as perceived by the decision-makers may not be equivalent to the influence as perceived by the observers; experimental research on attribution has demonstrated that there may even be some systematic perceptual differences between these groups (Jones and Nisbett 1971). Also, actors can actively influence others' perceptions of their responsibility by dramatizing their choices to a different extent. By making decisions which look like choices and displaying them for observers, individuals, or groups are able to acquire responsibility; by avoiding such decisions they can avoid responsibility.

This points to an important role for standard decision theory: by describing decision-making as procedures for choice, standard decision theory puts responsibility on the decision-makers. Since they have made a choice they must have had several alternative actions to choose from. By choosing one, they have established themselves as at least one important cause of that action. Therefore, whenever the standard theoretical conception of decision-making as choice is used for understanding actual decision-making, it tends to allocate responsibility to the decision-makers. When the ideas and ideals of standard decision theory are spread, it makes decisions produce responsibility.

There is, therefore, a paradoxical relation between the choice and the responsibility interpretations of decision-making: decision-making can work as a responsibility allocator only if observers perceive it as dealing with choice. The responsibility paradox may be one important reason why the choice interpretation of decision-making is popular—it is useful for producing both choice and responsibility.

The role of responsibility allocation has implications for the design of the decision process. If the decision process is to designate who is causing an action, it must clearly point out some persons. This means that the decision process as well as the decision-makers must be highly visible. The visibility of the final decision where the action to be realized is pointed out, is particularly important. Organizations often use specific procedures for making these final decisions which stress visibility, such as formal meetings with minutes telling what decisions were made by whom. Voting can be used not only as a way of finding out which alternative is preferred by most decision-makers but also for demonstrating exactly who is making the decision. Entering of reservations can serve the same purpose. The prominence of formal decisions is in sharp contrast to what can be expected from decision-making which serves the purpose of choice only; such decisions can be very difficult to observe—the discussions of alternatives sometimes transform into actions without any decision meeting or statement (Danielsson and Malmberg 1979).

If the decision process is to work as a responsibility allocator, it must also clearly establish the decision-makers as causes. It needs to produce the perception that the decision-makers have made a choice between two or more alternatives, and that they made the choice themselves and are personally and strongly connected to the alternative realized. The decision process must give the impression that a choice has been made but the procedure may well look irrational: the decision-makers' personal connection to the action to be realized is increased the more they stress their preference for it. This can be done by focusing on positive consequences only and by inventing general goals and values that fit the action.

Responsibility can also be established by arguments. Decision-makers can claim not only that they were among those who made a decision but also that they had influence on what was decided, that they actually made a choice. Their responsibility can also be reinforced by arguments—such arguments stress that it is the decision-makers' own values, beliefs, and perceptions that determine the decision and that determining values, beliefs, and perceptions are not objective, automatic, or controlled by others.

All these methods can be used in reverse if decision-makers do not want responsibility. They can use rational decision procedures. Rational decision procedures easily produce uncertainty at the same time, as they can be used for demonstrating that uncertainty in public; in this way the decision-makers can demonstrate that they are not strongly attached to the alternative decided on and that the choice of one alternative is the result of logical—and therefore objective and impersonal—reasoning out from general goals and values. If these goals and values can be argued to be shared by many people the decision-makers' attachment is further reduced. At the extreme, decision-makers may reduce their responsibility by substituting formal calculative models and computer programmes for their own reasoning, thus demonstrating that they did not choose but the model or computer did (Brunsson and Malmer 1978).

Decision-makers may also evade responsibility by making the decision or their roles as decision-makers less visible, for instance by avoiding a formal decision ritual. They may evade responsibility by claiming that they were not participating in the decision; they may point out that they formed a minority, voted against the decision or entered reservations. Decision-makers can also try to show that they had no choice, that there was just one possible alternative. Even without using impersonal rationalistic models they can argue that they did not influence the decision, that they were compelled by external forces. Studies of city budgeting in economic stagnation (Brunsson and Rombach 1982) give rich examples of this technique.

City budgeting is a highly visible decision process and a budget decision equally highly visible. Leading politicians are clearly pointed out as the decision-makers. In periods of strong growth, the resulting responsibility may be a relatively light burden but when cutbacks have to be made it might be both wise and attractive to try to avoid responsibility, both for 'guardians' and 'spenders' in Wildavsky's terms (1975). In the cities studied, the leading politicians who played the role of the guardians of the treasury thought that cutbacks of money for different services were necessary for over all economic reasons, but they did not want to be responsible for such cutbacks. One strategy was to avoid making individual cutback decisions. They tried to delegate cutback decisions to lower levels, to the spenders, those who asked and argued for money for their departments. For instance, the guardians asked every department to reduce its expenses by a certain percentage per year without giving any advice on exactly how this should be done. The guardians argued that the reductions should be made by minor changes in service levels and by increasing efficiency. Such minor things were normally decided by managers at lower levels. By making the reduction percentage equal for everybody, the guardians even avoided making an active choice of how much each department had to cut down. The counter strategy from the spenders was to argue that minor reforms were impossible or unreasonable, and instead they proposed cutbacks that meant the closing down of whole offices or programmes. Important decisions such as discontinuing services were normally made by the top, that is, the guardians. The spenders hoped (as it appeared, correctly) that the guardians would not make discontinuing decisions, since such decisions would give the guardians too much responsibility for strongly negative and highly visible actions.

Thus, what decisions were proposed and made was influenced not only by the decision-makers' preferences but also by the responsibility allocation effects of different decisions. In addition, responsibility was allocated by arguments describing decisions as choices or not. The guardians described their situation as one of no choice—they were forced by economic facts or the national government to cut down, they did not want it themselves. By just tranferring the figure of necessary expense reductions to all departments equally, they argued that they made no choice as to the distribution of cutbacks over departments. The spenders argued that even if there were externally determined necessities, the guardians had made a choice when they decided to cut down on a specific department—they could have chosen other distributions than the equal one. The spenders' arguments had the purpose of demonstrating that the guardians were making or intending to make decisions, involving choices, on highly negative actions and they tried to make these decisions highly visible.

The amount of responsibility residing with one decision-maker can also be affected by the total number of decision-makers—it may be diluted to different extents. The greater the number of decision-makers who have responsibility for an action, the less is the share of each decision-maker. If there is only one decision-maker, he or she carries all the responsibility but if everyone is responsible, no one is: in public referenda, to take an extreme, the vote of one individual normally does not change the majority, so there is no individual who is responsible, only more abstract entities such as the majority or the electorate. Responsibility can also be diluted over time; by splitting up one major decision into a series of minor ones, the amount of responsibility for each decision is reduced.

One of Sweden's largest industrial investments in the last decade was decided on by a process involving strong responsibility dilution over both organization and time (Brunsson 1983). Due to its heavy financial needs it had to pass through one company board, one corporate board, the national government, and the parliament. In addition, the decision was divided into a series of subsections, each one concerning further investigations or investments involving relatively minor costs or expressed in conditional form (such as 'we accept if others do'). Each decision-making unit then made several decisions at different points in time. The responsibility for each such small decision was easier to accept than the responsibility for the decision to make the whole investment. There was no single decision to make the investment.

Thus the investment could be made, although almost all the decision-makers were very sceptical or even negative about it. The investment turned out to be an economic disaster but afterwards neither those involved nor external observers were able to point to anyone having any considerable responsibility for it.

IMPLICATIONS FOR DECISION-MAKERS

In the choice and action perspectives the decision-makers are given the attractive role of affecting future actions without being affected themselves. The vast propagation of the theory of choice can be assumed to have increased the popularity of decision-making positions and processes. However, when consideration is given to the fact that decisions tend to affect the decision-makers by making them responsible, the decision-maker's role appears a less attractive one. When the success of the action to be decided on is uncertain, responsibility may be perceived as a negative quality of decisions. Whenever decision-makers consider the balance of influence on actions and responsibility for them to be unfair, they have incentives to try to change the balance or to leave their roles. The responsibility aspect sometimes explains why individuals or groups refrain from participating in decision-making. But decision-oriented organizations can seldom avoid decisions—they are expected to make some—and so they easily become responsible.

For the governments and boards studied, the responsibility aspect seemed to be more important than the choice aspect. This was evident in the city budgeting case where responsibility was avoided by affecting the content of the budget. Many indicators suggest that responsibility rather than choice was the normal result of the decisions made by the organizations studied. Most of their decisions were made highly visible by a series of techniques: the decision-makers made clear that they made decisions and what these were, minutes where the decisions were listed were prepared and in the governments' case information about decisions was actively spread among the public by these protocols, by opening meetings to the public, or by other channels. By voting or reservations it was made clear who made the decisions. The decisions were preceded by processes through which they appeared as choices—discussions of problems, preferences, alternatives, and consequences. External observers such as the press or people affected by the decisions described the decision-makers as influential—the decision-makers were supposed to have influenced the content of the decision, at least as long as they belonged to the majority. But the organizations concentrated on making the final decision; other parts of the decision proccess were delegated to others. Experts, administrators, or special committees investigated preferences, alternatives, and consequences and the same or other groups were to implement the decisions. The important choices were normally made before the issue reached the decision-makers or the alternatives were formulated in a way that made the choice obvious—for instance one and only one alternative fitted the majority. Other studies of similar organizations demonstrate that choices can be made after the decision, for instance when decisions are formulated so vaguely as to permit a wide array of subsequent actions (Baier, March, and Saetren 1986).

These observations are not unique. There is ample research showing that boards and councils making formal decisions often have little influence on the decisions' content—this has been determined during the preparation of the decisions by experts (Brunsson and Jönsson 1979). In spite of this fact, members of boards and councils seldom officially complain that they lack influence. In the organizations studied no decision-maker tried to alter the public picture of them as influential, even though some of them complained about their lack of influence in private discussions with the author.

Even if the decisions are not influencing the choice of alternatives to any important extent, they are publicly presented as both aiming at and resulting in choices. Any glance at management or political science textbooks reveals that decision-oriented organizations are expected to make choices and exert influence. This discrepancy between presentation and actual behaviour can be explained by the responsibility paradox: if you claim influence, you will get responsibility. Decision-makers and decision-making units who are anxious to fill their role as responsibility acceptors must argue that they had influence on the choice. Those who argue that they had no influence actually communicate that they did not cause the action decided and thus have no responsibility for it. Whatever their actual influence, decision-makers must be considered influential if they are to be responsible. Participation in decision-making processes is supposed to give influence. Giving organizations the power to make decisions is to give them the ability to absorb responsibility. The choice perspective is used as an argument for employees' participation in decision-making processes oriented towards the achievement of industrial democracy or for politicians' decision-making in political democracies; the purpose of the politicians' role as decision-makers or the unions' participation in management decisions is often described as being to give these groups influence on what actions are chosen. The responsibility aspect of decision-making makes it equally possible to interpret these appointments as attempts to place responsibility on the group in question, for instance giving unions responsibility for necessary restructurings of industries and thereby smoothing their completion.

By making some organizations, groups, or individuals absorb responsibility, the responsibility of others can be reduced or deleted, and the decision-makers become potential scapegoats or heroes. Decisions can thus serve as instruments for control; they make clear to whom should be given rewards or punishments and this can be used for influencing people's decisions. When their decisions affect actions, for instance by choosing them, action can be controlled in this way. The notion of a fair balance between responsibility and influence is important also for controllers; if decision-makers are not influential, the control of decision-makers is futile and if influential people are not decision-makers and thereby responsible, they may be difficult to control.

IMPLICATIONS FOR ACTION

Responsibility provides a link between actions and decision-makers. It not only affects the decision-maker but also the actions. Actions may be affected by being given legitimacy: by making decisions and accepting responsibility decision-makers with a high degree of personal or role legitimacy provide actions with legitimacy. For example, politicians decide on many actions of administrating subunits, thereby making them socially legitimate. Such legitimation is important if highly controversial actions are to be completed. By making the decision and sticking to it in spite of criticism and protests from the environment, the politicians protect the administration and its action from the turbulence of the environment, for instance from changes in social values and factual conditions. This is particularly important for actions that are long-term and difficult to change once started. Local politicians have argued that having a tough skin is one of their most important qualities (Brunsson and Jönsson 1979).

Decisions may also provide events with meaning. By allocating responsibility, decisions meet the need of human beings to explain why things happen, a need which is fundamental for humankind (Geertz 1973). In western secularized culture it is important to establish people rather than nature, chance or God as causes of events. This is exactly what decisions do. This can explain why decisions are sometimes made about events that the decision-makers cannot possibly influence, for instance when governments make decisions about unsolvable problems such as drug abuse or business cycles. In traditional African societies witchcraft and 'witch-detectives' are used for exaggerating the responsibility of persons for unfortunate events (Gluckman 1972). In western societies politics and politicians may play a similar role.

The responsibility results of decisions can be used for linking the organization to parts of its environment. Organizations may decide about events and actions in their environment, thereby accepting responsibility for them. Western national governments have been observed to deal with more and more societal issues. Their main way of dealing with the issues is to make decisions—about payments of money, about resources to public administration units, or about laws. By these decisions they may not only become responsible for the actions of the public sector but also for the results of these actions and thereby for what happens in the environment. If organizations decide about areas which are generally perceived favourably—or that become favourable due to the organizations' actions—they may gain legitimacy; governments spending money in prospering industries demonstrate that they are responsible for success. If organizations decide about areas which are perceived as negative in spite of the actions they decide on, they may transfer some of their legitimacy to the area. A national government studied, decided to launch a very expensive programme with the official motive of solving severe unemployment problems in a region. However, the decision-makers privately did not believe that the problem would be solved and they did not find this important. Instead, they considered themselves to have accepted responsibility for the situation and thereby influenced the attitudes of people in the region who were now thought of as perceiving their (unchanged) situation less pressing.

Decisions may also serve as more direct instruments for affecting organizational legitimacy. This is the topic of the next section.

DECISIONS AS LEGITIMATION

A common denomination of all three aspects of decisions discussed earlier is that, in different ways, they connect decisions and actions. Actions are chosen, mobilized, or given responsibility for by decision-making and decisions. But sometimes decision-making may not be connected to actions at all. There is ample evidence that decisions often are not followed by actions or that subsequent actions are not in sympathy with previous decisions. Such differences between decisions and actions are often described as problems of implementation; decision-makers have not been able to force other people to behave as decided and this causes problems for the decision-makers and the organization (Pressman and Wildavsky 1973; Mayntz 1976). A disconnection between a decision and action need not be interpreted as a problem, however; it can also be interpreted as a solution, as will be discussed below.

Organizational actions constitute one output of organizations which can provide legitimacy and support for the organization in its environment as long as the actions reflect the values and norms prevalent in that environment (Parsons 1956). But decisions can also be considered organizational outputs; many organizations are anxious to publicly declare some of their decisions. If these decisions reflect external norms, they can serve as independent instruments for external legitimation. Many decision-oriented organizations such as parliaments, councils, and governments even specialize in producing decisions and refrain from producing organizational actions at all.

If environmental norms are inconsistent with each other, organizations can act according to some norms and decide according to others, thereby reflecting a large part of external norms. This behaviour produces inconsistencies between decisions and actions but these inconsistencies are solutions rather than problems; solutions to the problem of maintaining and gaining external legitimacy and support when external norms are inconsistent. Such decisions deal with uncertainty related to organizational legitimacy rather than uncertainty related to alternatives, actions, or decision-makers. The literature on implementation problems reports many inconsistencies between the decisions made by parliaments, councils, and governments on different levels and actions taken by public administration units. This is no coincidence. Such organizations typically have to deal with many inconsistent norms (Edelman 1971) and they may accomplish this by letting some units specialize in decision-making and others in action. Decisions can then reflect some norms and action others. Decisions can compensate for action. Rombach (1986) found that cities facing stagnation decided to rationalize their activities in order to decrease expenditures, but he found no such rationalizations carried out. Instead, expenditures were increased and expansion continued.

When used as legitimating devices, formal decisions must be clearly visible to the environment. When organizations use decisions in this way, they can be expected to be anxious to publish their decisions. But organizations do not only produce actions and decisions. A third organizational output is talk—the spoken and written word with which the organization presents itself to its environment (Brunsson 1986). Talk can be inconsistent with both decisions and actions, and compensate for them in situations of inconsistent norms. For instance, the most extensive socialization of Swedish industry was made during a short period of liberal governments propagating ideas of free markets and less state intervention after forty-four years of socialist governments. Also, socialist governments have been observed to carry out relatively easily conservative policies such as fighting inflation by reducing wage increases.

Decisions can also be a rationale for producing talk; they can be described and explained. In situations where inconsistent norms prevail, different descriptions of the same decision may be inconsistent and explanations of the decisions to the public may be inconsistent with their contents as described in protocols. In these situations it is very clear that a decision has been made, but it is unclear exactly what the decision is; the decision is both evident and equivocal.

Talk can also be produced by the process preceding the decision. This provides a reason for organizations to make not only their decisions but also their decision processes public. The purpose of reflecting norms may influence the design of the decision process. Different norms are consistent with different preferences, alternatives, and consequences. Rational decision processes where many preferences, alternatives, and consequences are considered are therefore better instruments for reflecting inconsistent norms than more irrational ones. Again, budgeting in public sector organizations is an example in point. There the decision process is typically open to the public and the struggle between spenders and guardians displays a great many conflicting preferences, alternatives, and consequences.

THE FOUR ROLES OF DECISION

In this chapter, four interpretations of organizational decision-making and decisions have been put forward (Table 2.1). It has been argued that the role of decision-making can be not only choice and the mobilization of organizational action but also responsibility allocation and organizational legitimation. Decision-making can reduce uncertainty related to alternatives, actors, decision-makers, or legitimacy. Decision-makers may adapt the design of decision-making processes to these different roles and to what the decision-makers want to achieve within the role. Different designs as to the degrees of visibility and rationality have different implications for the four roles, and different degrees of rationality provide more or less need for accounting information. For instance, if accounting information is used more for defensive than for offensive decisions (Häckner 1985), the reason may be that defensive decisions serve purposes that need more rationality. When decisions are highly formal and visible there are reasons for interpreting them as dealing with more or other aspects than choice. The extent to which decision processes follow the rational norms of standard decision theory should be expected to vary according to their role and the purpose of the decision-makers. A high degree of rationality can be interpreted as an attempt to solve the problem of choice, to prevent or stop organizational action, to evade responsibility, or to legitimate the organization in an environment where inconsistent norms are important. Rationality provides a distance between decision and action: rational decision-making deals with choice rather than mobilization, it decouples decision-makers from actions and it legitimates in situations where inconsistencies between the decision and actions are favourable.

Table 2.1. Four roles of decisions

Role	Choice	Mobilization	Responsibility allocation	Legitimation
Handle uncertainty as to	Alternatives	Commitments	Decision-makers	Organizational legitimacy
Connection to actions	Connected	Connected	Connected	Disconnected
Design	Rationality	Irrationality	Irrationality for responsibility acceptance	Rationality in environments of inconsistent norms

A high degree of irrationality is not necessarily a result of decision-makers failing to make a rational choice—it can also be interpreted as an attempt to create strong commitment, to accept more responsibility or to legitimate the organization in relation to a group of consistent norms. Irrationality produces a strong connection between decisions and actions—it mobilizes and it ties decision-makers to action, and is useful for legitimation in situations when consistent norms apply, making consistency between decisions and actions important.

In practice, decision processes may play more than one of the roles described here, sometimes all four. Different or the same decision-makers may want to use decision processes for different purposes or, whatever their own preferences, decision-makers may be aware of observers interpreting the processes in several ways. Budgeting or other decision processes may even involve a battle between groups trying to establish it as playing one role or another. Such decision processes may become very complicated and seem extremely fuzzy both for participants and external observers and they are not possible to understand if analysed from the perspective of one role only.

The four roles of decisions affect not only the design but also the number of decisions. They not only indicate four different benefits of decisions but also point out four different possible costs. Potential decision-makers may avoid decision-making since they expect it to lead to the choice of an alternative that they do not wish, to too weak a mobilization or a demobilization, to responsibility being placed on the wrong persons, or to a loss of organizational legitimacy; and since they realize that there exist other means for making choices, for mobilizing, for responsibility allocation and for legitimating. Therefore, there is not always a need for making decisions, nor is there always a capacity for making them. The number of decisions can be affected by such things as the prevalance of rules, talk, and products.

Choices can be made by reference to existing rules rather than by decisions where future consequences are considered. A large number of organizational actions are chosen by rules at different levels of abstraction, from assembly lines by which individual hand movements are prescribed to organizational ideologies which constitute shared ways of perceiving and interpreting even new situations and events occurring within the organization or its environment. Organizations that maintain many and strong rules have less need for decision-making as a way of choosing. Organizations that breed strong ideologies are able to make choices without decisions even in situations which are new for the organization (Brunsson 1985). Rules are also means for mobilizing organizational actions—they can provide as much motivation and expectation as decisions can and commitment can be formed by other processes than by decision processes. This is true also for hierarchy:

organizations where direct orders from the top are highly legitimate do not need decision-processes as a means for mobilizing action.

Rules can also affect the number of decisions by reducing the capacity for benefiting from decisions. If there are many and strong rules, it is difficult to use decisions for choice, for accepting responsibility or for gaining legitimacy; the rules will control the choice and the rules rather than decision-makers will be connected to actions.

Similarly, the need for using decisions as legitimating devices is dependent on the organization's ability or possibility for using other legitimating instruments. Organizations that have problems in creating or maintaining legitimacy by their products or by talk become more dependent on decisions as legitimating devices. For instance, most decision-oriented organizations do not produce any products and it may be difficult to make people listen to their talk if they do not produce decisions (Rombach 1986). Also, responsibility, whether desired or not, may be obtained without decisions—some organizations have societal positions which give them responsibility without their having made active decisions, as the debate on corporate responsibility tells us (Epstein and Votaw 1978). A capacity for decisions may produce a need for them. Organizations that are perceived as being able to make decisions in specific areas can become responsible for events even without making decisions about them. By making decisions instead they have greater chances to influence exactly what they are to be responsible for. Governments given responsibility for the economic situation in the country may be better off by making some positively perceived decisions about it (Brunsson 1986).

The variety of roles that decision-making can play has implications for both descriptive and normative research. They can be used not only for better understanding of decision processes but also for gaining a better insight into the roles and behaviour of decision-oriented organizations. Boards, parliaments, and governments are often supposed to be highly important for other people or organizations or for society at large. If this assumption is true, a better understanding of their decision-making becomes fundamental for understanding these larger systems.

The choice interpretation of decision-making has led to recommendations of rationality, while the other interpretations of decision-making suggest that irrationality sometimes should be recommended. Organizations must often be advised not to use rational decision models or calculation techniques, like those produced by operations research, or not to use accounting information too extensively or in an unbiased way. They can also be advised to continue emphasizing budgeting procedures, even if these have not produced the right choices, if responsibility and legitimacy are more important. The choice interpretation has also implied recommendations to those who want to influence actions that they should create decision-making processes preceding action and that they should secure their own participation in these processes. The other interpretations lead to warnings that decision-making procedures may not be useful for gaining influence or may cost too much responsibility to be worthwhile. People who want influence cannot always be advised to establish themselves as decision-makers, in particular if they are not ready to pay the costs of responsibility. Both descriptive and normative research should investigate decision designs that promote not only choice but also the other roles of decision processes and, of course, explore ways other than decisions for producing organizational choice, mobilization, responsibility, and legitimacy.

REFERENCES

Aristotle (1984). *The Nichomachean Ethics*. Oxford: Oxford University Press.

Baier, E., March, J., and Saetren, H. (1986) 'Implementation and Ambiguity', *Scandinavian Journal of Management Studies*, 197–212.

Barnard, C. (1938). *The Functions of the Executive*. Cambridge, MA: Harvard University Press.

Brunsson, N. (1982). 'The Irrationality of Action and Action Rationality: Decisions, Ideologies and Organizational Actions', *Journal of Management Studies*, 29–44.

———— (1983). *Projektinstitutionalisering—ett fall*. Stockholm: EFI.

———— (1985). *The Irrational Organization*. Chichester, UK: Wiley.

———— (1986). 'Organizing for Inconsistencies. On Organizational Conflict, Depressions and Hypocrisy as Substitutes for Action', *Scandinavian Journal of Management Studies*, 165–85.

———— and Jönsson, S. (1979). *Beslut och Handling*. Stockholm: Liber.

———— and Malmer, S. (1978). *Värdering av produktutvecklingsprojekt*. Göteborg: Göteborgs Universitet.

———— and Rombach, B. (1982). *Går det att spara*. Lund: Doxa.

Cohen, M., March, J. and Olsen, J. (1972). 'A Garbage Can Model of Rational Choice', *Administration Science Quarterly*, 1–25.

Danielsson, A. and Malmberg, A. (1979). *Beslut fattas*. Stockholm: SAF.

Edelman, M. (1971). *Politics as Symbolic Action*. New York: Academic Press.

Edwards, R. (1969). *Freedom, Responsibility and Obligation*. The Hague: Martinus Nijhoff.

Epstein, E. and Votaw, D. (1978). *Rationality, Legitimacy and Responsibility*. Santa Monica: Goodyear.

Fayol, H. (1949). *General and Industrial Management*, 2nd edn. London: Pitman.

Fincham, F. and Jaspars, J. (1980). 'Attribution of Responsibility: From Man the Scientist to Man as Lawyer', in L. Berkowitz (ed.), *Advances in Experimental and Social Psychology*. New York: Academic Press.

French, P. (1984). *Collective and Corporate Responsibility*. New York: Columbia University Press.

Geertz, C. (1973). *The Interpretation of Cultures*. New York: Basic Books.

Gluckman, M. (1972). 'Moral Crises: Magical and Secular Solutions', in M. Gluckman (ed.), *The Allocation of Responsibility*. Manchester, UK: Manchester University Press.

Helkama, K. (1981). *Toward a Cognitive Developmental Theory of Attribution of Responsibility*. Helsinki: Suomalainen Tiedeakatemia.

Huysmans, J. H. (1970). 'The Effectiveness of the Cognitive Style Constraint in Implementing Operations Research Proposals', *Management Science*, 99–103.

Häckner, E. (1985). *Strategiutveckling i medelstora företag*. Göteborg: BAS.

Jones, E. and Nisbett, R. (1971). 'The Actor and the Observer: Divergent Perceptions of the Causes of Behaviour', in E. Jones et al. (eds.), *Attribution*. Morristown: General Learning Press.

Kahneman, D. and Tversky, A. (1973). 'On the Psychology of Prediction', *Psychological Review*, 237–51.

Kelley, H. (1972). 'Attribution in Social Interaction', in E. Jones, et al. (eds.), *Attribution*. Morristown: General Learning Press.

March, J. (1976). 'The Technology of Foolishness', in J. March and J. Olsen (eds.), *Ambiguity and Choice in Organizations*. Bergent, Norway: Universitetsforlaget.

March, J. and Simon, H. (1958). *Organizations*. New York: Wiley.

Mayntz, R. (1976) 'Environmental Policy Conflicts: The Case of the German Federal Republic', *Policy Analysis*, 557–87.

Nisbett, R. and Ross, L. (1980). *Human Inference*. Englewood Cliffs, NJ: Prentice-Hall.

Parsons, T. (1956). 'Suggestions for a Sociological Approach to the Theory of Organization', *Administrative Science Quarterly*, 63–85.

Pressman, J. and Wildavsky, A. (1973). *Implementation*. Berkeley, CA: University of California Press.

Rombach, B. (1986). *Rationalisering eller prat?* Lund, Sweden: Doxa.

Ross, A. (1975). *On Guilt, Responsibility and Punishment*. London: Stevens.

Simon, H. (1965). *Administrative Behavior*, 2nd edn. New York: The Free Press.

Spiro, H. (1969). *Responsibility in Government: Theory and Practice*. New York: Van Nostrand Reinhold.

Swieringa, R. and Weick, K. (1987). 'Management Accounting and Action', *Accounting, Organizations and Society*, 293–308.

Wildavsky, A. (1975). *Budgeting*. Boston, MA: Little, Brown.

3

The Irrationality of Action and Action Rationality: Decisions, Ideologies, and Organizational Actions

> Thus conscience does make cowards of us all;
> And thus the native hue of resolution
> Is sicklied o'er with the pale cast of thought,
> And enterprises of great pitch and moment,
> With this regard, their currents turn awry
> And lose the name of action
>
> (*Hamlet*, Act III)

THE DECISION-MAKING PERSPECTIVE AND IRRATIONALITY

A characteristic of social science is the multitude perspectives used by different researchers. The significant differences between research fields lie less often in what is described than in how it is described. One important way of developing a social science is to apply new perspectives to a part of reality, thereby highlighting new features of the reality. Perspectives determine what data are seen, what theories are developed, and what kinds of results turn up.

One of the most influential perspectives has been the decision-making perspective which conceives of human behaviour as resulting from decisions made by individuals, groups, or organizations. A decision is normally described as a conscious choice between at least two alternative actions. Researchers have studied the choosing among alternatives, the generating of alternatives, and the forming of criteria for choice (goals, objectives).

The attractiveness of the decision-making perspective has several explanations. One explanation is that diverse social theories can be stated in decision-making terms. This is true for parts of microeconomics and of political science. Another explanation is that the perspective lends itself to experimentation; psychological researchers can create experimental decision situations by giving people objectives and information, and then they study the resulting choices. In addition, social development has spawned situations where the decision-making perspective seems relevant from a common-sense point of view. The establishment and growth of large organizations have added hierarchy to society and, consequently, many actions are determined by forces outside the actors themselves (Galbraith 1967; Chandler 1977; Lindblom 1977). This separates cognition from action and makes it natural to say some individuals decide and others carry out the decisions. The decision-making perspective seems almost imperative in democratic conventions. According to the existing law for industrial democracy in Sweden, for example, the employees' influence should be guaranteed by their participation in decisions. These imperatives may result from a spread of the decision-making perspective from researchers to practitioners.

Still, the decision-making perspective has been derived from studies of individual behaviour rather than organizational. An individual has less difficulty going from decision to action than does an organization. This emphasis on individual behaviour might explain why the choosing of actions has received much more attention than the carrying out of actions. Organizational decision processes are described in essentially the same terms as individual decision processes, and research has often characterized organizations as being led by single powerful entrepreneurs (as in microeconomic theory) or by coalitions (as described by Cyert and March 1963).

The decision-making perspective has been most elaborated in normative research which prescribes how decisions should be made. This kind of research sets the criteria for a 'rational' decision. Strong efforts have been devoted to prescribing how a best choice should be made, given a specific problem, specific alternatives, and specific information. Typically, a problem is described as one where there is either too little information or too much. Little attention has been paid to other phases of decision-making processes or to implementing the decisions made.

Normative research has engendered an increasing consensus among researchers as to what kinds of decision-making should be called rational. At the same time, empirical research has found ample evidence of decision-making processes that appear irrational by the normative standards (Lindblom 1959; Cyert and March 1963; Janis 1972; Tversky and Kahneman 1974; March and Olsen 1976; Nisbett and Ross 1980). What is more, the apparent irrationalities are not limited to insignificant decisions: people behave similarly when making major decisions on strategic issues. It can even be argued that the apparent irrationalities are largest in major decisions. Janis (1972) demonstrated how decisions with serious actual or potential effects—such as the decision by the Kennedy administration to start the invasion in the Bay of Pigs—were made without normative rationality. Disturbing information was suppressed, and false illusions of unanimity were built up among the decision-makers, who took immense and unjustified risks.

There are three common ways of explaining the irrationality found in practice. One chauvinist explanation is that the people studied are not clever enough to behave rationally. For instance, difficulties of implementing models from operations research have been explained by managers' emotional reactions or by their cognitive styles (Tarkowsky 1958; Huysmans 1970). If decision-makers only had the brain capacities and knowledge of scientists, they would behave as the rational decision models prescribe. Thus, decision-makers ought to be selected and trained better.

A second explanation derives from psychological research, which indicates that certain types of irrationality are inherent characteristics of human beings, and these characteristics are difficult to change by training (Goldberg 1968; Kahneman and Tversky 1973). Consequently, not even experts can be fully rational, and full rationality can only be reached by mathematical formulae or computer programs.

A third way of explaining apparently irrational behaviour is to point out practical restrictions. In realistic decision situations, values, alternatives, and predictions interact; so decision-makers have incomplete information, or they have more information than human beings can grasp. This view implies that normative research should design systems for gathering and processing data. Not many years ago, some people expected computer-based information systems to solve numerous management problems (Murdick and Ross 1975). Also, recognizing that objectives may be difficult to compare with each other, normative research has produced cost–benefit analysis and multiple-criteria methods (Prest and Turvey 1965; Keeney and Raiffa 1976).

These traditional explanations are made within the decision-making perspective. They refer to diverse phenomena that disturb decision processes. Like the decision processes themselves, the disturbances are described as being cognitive; they arise from deficiencies in perceived information or deficiencies in decision-makers' mental abilities.

These ways of explaining irrationality cannot be said to be inherently wrong, but there is much evidence that these explanations do not suffice. Computer-based information systems have not been used in the prescribed ways; recommendations given by operations-research models have not been followed; cost–benefit analyses have not been done or have been neglected even by competent and successful managers and politicians (Churchman 1964; Harvey 1970; Ackerman et al. 1974; Argyris 1977).

If actual behaviour is to be understood, other explanations are needed. As long as actual behaviour is not fully understood, the recommendations of normative research may be irrelevant, confusing, or even harmful.

The main purpose of this chapter is to argue that an action perspective will be more fruitful for understanding large areas of organizational behaviour. The action perspective explains behaviour within attempts to change and differences in abilities to achieve changes. Because organizational actions do not lend themselves to laboratory experiments, the chapter is based on studies of major organizational changes or stabilities in seven organizations. The organizations include industrial companies, governmental agencies, and local governments. Processes of change were observed, and people's ways of describing both the changes and the general situations were measured.

The decision-making perspective fails to recognize that practitioners do more than make decisions. Making a decision is only a step towards action. A decision is not an end product. Practitioners get things done, act and induce others to act.

An action perspective makes it easier and important to observe that there exist both decisions without actions and actions without decisions. Some actions are not preceded by weighing of objectives, evaluating of alternatives, or choosing; and decision processes and decisions do not always influence actions, particularly not when the actions precede the decisions. On the other hand, decision processes often comprise some of the processes associated with actions. Because managers and representatives in political bodies describe part of their work as decision-making, decisions and decision-making should remain important topics for study.

In fact, the very relationship between decision-making and action helps explain why decisions deviate from normative rationality. Since decision processes aim at action, they should not be designed solely according to such decision-internal criteria as the norms of rationality; they should be adapted to external criteria of action. Rational decisions are not always good bases for appropriate and successful actions.

How can decisions lay foundations for actions? The next section attempts to answer this question.

DECISIONS AS INITIATORS OF ACTIONS

Making decisions is just one way among several of initiating actions in organizations. However, it is a familiar one. Actions are often preceded by group activities which the participants describe as decision-making steps. Certain issues are posed in forms that allow them to be handled by decision processes: several alternative actions are proposed, their probable effects are forecasted, and finally actions are chosen. Sometimes the decision-makers even formulate goals or other explicit criteria by which the alternatives can be evaluated. The final results are called decisions.

For decisions to initiate actions, they must incorporate cognitive, motivational, and committal aspects. One cognitive aspect of a decision is expectation: the decision expresses the expectation that certain actions will take place. A decision also demonstrates motivation to take action, and it expresses the decision-makers' commitments to specific actions. By making a decision, decision-makers accept responsibility both for getting the actions carried out and for the appropriateness of the actions.

To go from decision to action is particularly complicated and difficult when there are several decision-makers and several actors and when decision-makers and actors are different persons. These conditions are typical of organizations. Thus, organizations should provide motivational and social links from decisions to actions. Strong motivations, sometimes even enthusiasm, are needed to overcome big intellectual or physical obstacles. Cooperating actors should be able to rely on certain kinds of behaviours and attitudes from their collaborators, so they should construct mutual commitments: the actors should signal to one another that they endorse proposed actions, for example, by presenting arguments in favour of them or by expressing confidence in success. Actors should also elicit commitments from those who will evaluate their actions afterwards, because committed evaluators are more likely to judge actions as successful (Brunsson 1976).

Thinking, motivation, and commitment are aspects of all actions. However, the importance of each aspect might differ in various situations, depending on such variables as the actors' time horizons, the degrees of change that the actions involve, and the power relationships within the organization. Cognitive activities probably become more important where the actors expect more information to be beneficial. Motivations would be more important where actors lack information needed for predicting the consequences of acting, where the negative consequences could be great, or where great efforts are essential; motivations would be less important where the actions are highly complex and the actors must collaborate extensively (Zander 1971). Commitments would be more important where many people are involved in actions, agreements from many people are necessary, efforts must be tightly coordinated, or results depend upon the actions or evaluations of collaborators who are accessible through communication. Since motivations and commitments represent internal pressures for action, they are particularly influential where external pressures are weak. This is true of wait-and-see situations where people think that it may be possible to take no action: the actors can reject one proposed action without having to accept another at the same time.

The stronger the expectation, motivation, and commitment expressed in a decision, the more power that decision exerts as a basis for action. In so far as the constituents of decisions are determined by decision processes, the likelihoods of actions can be influenced by designing the decision processes. However, effective decision processes break nearly all the rules for rational decision-making: few alternatives should be analysed, only positive consequences of the chosen actions should be considered, and objectives should not be formulated in advance.

The following subsections explain how irrationalities can build good bases for organizational actions.

Searching for Alternatives

According to the rational model, all possible alternatives should be evaluated. This is impossible, so the injunction is often reformulated as evaluating as many alternatives as possible.

In reality, it seems easier to find decision processes which consider few alternatives (typically two) than ones which consider many alternatives. It is even easy to find decision processes which consider only one alternative. This parsimony makes sense from an action point of view, because considering multiple alternatives evokes uncertainty, and uncertainty reduces motivation and commitment. If actors are uncertain whether a proposed action is good, they are less willing to undertake it and to commit themselves to making it succeed. For example, in order to facilitate product development projects, uncertainty should not be analysed but avoided (Brunsson 1980). If people do not know which action will actually be carried out, they have to build up motivations for several alternatives at the same time, and this diffuses the motivations supporting any single alternative. For the same reasons, commitments may be dispersed or destroyed by the consideration of several alternatives. Therefore, very early in decision processes, if possible before the processes even start, decision-makers should get rid of alternatives that have weak to moderate chances of being chosen.

On the other hand, alternatives with no chance of being chosen do not have these negative effects: they may even reinforce motivation and commitment. One strategy is to propose alternatives which are clearly unacceptable but which highlight by comparison the virtues of an acceptable alternative. This defines the situation as not being of the wait-and-see type: rejecting one alternative means accepting another. Another and more important effect is that commitments become double-sided: commitments arise not only through endorsements of acceptable alternatives but also through criticisms of unacceptable alternatives. Thus, considering two alternatives can lay a stronger foundation for action than considering only one alternative if one of the two alternatives is clearly unacceptable.

One example is the decision process following the merger of Sweden's three largest steel companies. The merger was supposed to make production more efficient by concentrating each kind of production in one steelworks. A six-month-long decision process considered several alternative ways of redistributing production. Besides the alternative that was actually chosen, however, only one alternative was investigated thoroughly. This was the alternative to make no change at all. Because this alternative would have made the merger meaningless, no one considered it a practical action.

Estimating Consequences

Decision-makers who want to make rational decisions are supposed to consider all relevant consequences that alternatives might have; positive and negative consequences should get equal attention. But such a procedure evokes much uncertainty, for inconsistent information produces bewilderment and doubt, and stimulates conflicts among decision-makers (Hoffman 1968). Also, it is difficult to weigh positive and negative consequences together (Slovic 1966).

One way of avoiding uncertainty is to search for consequences in only one direction—to seek support for the initial opinion about an alternative. People tend to anchor their judgements in the first cues they perceive (Slovic 1972; Tversky and Kahneman 1974). Searching for positive consequences of an acceptable alternative has high priority, while negative consequences are suppressed. The purpose is not only to avoid uncertainty: active search for arguments in favour of an alternative also helps to create enthusiasm and to increase commitments. If negative consequences do pop up, adding more positive consequences can at least help to maintain commitment and motivation.

For example, in a company with high propensity to undertake innovative product development projects, personnel spent most of their discussions collecting arguments in favour of specific projects. This helped them to build up enthusiasm for projects—an enthusiasm that they deemed necessary to overcome difficulties (Brunsson 1976).

Evaluating Alternatives

The rational model prescribes that alternatives and their consequences should be evaluated according to predetermined criteria, preferably in the form of objectives. Decision-makers are told to start with objectives and then to find out what effects the alternatives would have on them. This is a dangerous strategy from the action point of view because there is a high risk that decision-makers will formulate inconsistent objectives and will have difficulties assessing alternatives. Data are needed that are difficult or impossible to find, and different pieces of information may point in conflicting directions.

For producing action, a better strategy is to start from the consequences and to invent the objectives afterwards (Lindblom 1959). Predicted consequences are judged to be good because they can be reformulated as desirable objectives. The relations between alternatives and objectives are not investigated in detail, only enough to demonstrate some positive links. The objectives are arguments, not criteria for choice; they are instruments for motivation and commitment, not for investigation. The argumentative role of objectives becomes evident in situations where objectives are abandoned after data indicate that they will not be promoted by preferred actions.

For instance, the calculations in the merged steel company actually demonstrated that the no-change alternative would be at least as profitable as the alternative that was chosen. The decision-makers then shifted their criterion from profitability as defined in the calculations to criteria such as access to a harbour and the age of a steelworks—criteria which favoured the alternative to be chosen.

Choosing

Within the decision-making perspective, a decision is normally described as a choice which follows automatically from preceding analysis. But when decision-making initiates action, a choice is not merely a statement of preference for one alternative but an expression of commitment to carrying out an action. A choice can be formulated in diverse ways which express different degrees of commitment and enthusiasm: which people participate in choosing influences, which people participate in acting.

A local government with an unstable majority postponed for eight years a decision about where to build new houses. Yet, at every time, there existed a majority favouring one location. Majority support was not thought to be a sufficient basis for the complicated and time-consuming planning work to follow (Brunsson 1981; Jönsson 1982).

Making Rational use of Irrationality

The purpose of action calls for irrationality. Some irrationalities are consistent with the prescriptions of Lindblom (1959) who argued that thorough rational analyses are irrelevant for the incremental steps in American national policy. But irrationality is even more valuable for actions involving radical changes, because motivation and commitment are crucial.

Much of the decision irrationality observed in decision processes can be explained as action rationality. The hypothesis that such may be the case is worth considering at least in situations where motivation and commitment are highly beneficial. For example, this kind of explanation can be applied to some of the strategic decisions described by Janis (1972). Much of the irrationality Janis observed in the decision of the Kennedy administration to invade Cuba can be explained by the fact that such risky and normally illegitimate actions needed extreme motivation and commitment to be adopted. Strong motivations and commitments seem actually to have arisen, and they led to very strong efforts to complete the action in spite of great difficulties and uncertainties.

According to Janis, better alternatives would have been found if the decision process had been more rational, giving room for more criticism, alternative perspectives, and doubts. Perhaps so. But deciding more rationally in order to avoid big failures is difficult advice to follow. If the decisions should initiate actions, the irrationality is functional and should not be replaced by more rational decision procedures. Rational analyses are more appropriate where motivation and commitment offer weak benefits. This is true for actions which are less significant, less complicated, and short term. Lundberg (1961) observed that investment calculations are made for small, marginal investments but not for large, strategic ones. If one believes that rational decision processes lead to better choices, this observation should be disquieting. Moreover, important actions tend to be carried out with strong motivations and commitments, which make it difficult to stop or change directions if the actions prove to be mistakes.

There is also the opposite risk—that decision rationality impedes difficult but necessary actions. For actions involving major organizational changes, the magnitudes of the issues and the uncertainties involved may frighten people into making analyses as carefully as possible. At the same time, the uncertainty potentials and the involvements of many people heighten the risks that rational decision-making will obstruct action.

One extreme and pathological case of decision-making giving no basis for action is decision orientation This occurs when people regard decision-making as their only activity, not caring about the actions, and not even presuming that there will be actions. In full accordance with the decision-making perspective, these people look upon decisions as end points. In one political organization, for instance, the politicians facilitated their decision-making substantially by concentrating on making decisions and ignoring subsequent actions. Since the decisions were not to be carried out, the politicians did not have to worry about negative effects, and they could easily reach agreements. On the other hand, the lack of actions threatened the survival of the organization.

To sum up, rational decision-making procedures fulfil the function of choice—they lead to the selection of action alternatives. But organizations face two problems: to choose the right thing to do and to get it done. There are two kinds of rationality, corresponding to these two problems: decision rationality and action rationality. The one is not better than the other, but they serve different purposes and imply different norms. The two kinds of rationality are difficult to pursue simultaneously because rational decision-making procedures are irrational from an action perspective; they should be avoided if actions are to be facilitated.

How can the problems of choice and of action be solved concurrently? One way is to solve the problem of choice by means of ideologies instead of by decisions. Ideologies can fulfil the function of choice without impeding actions. This is the theme of the next section.

IDEOLOGIES THAT FACILITATE ACTIONS

Recent research has stressed other cognitive aspects of organizational life than decision-making. Organizational members share interests which determine their participation in an organization. They also perceive similarly the organization, its environment, its history, and its future. Some shared knowledge, perspectives, and attitudes persist over time (Clark 1972; Starbuck 1976; Jönsson and Lundin 1977; Starbuck, Greve, and Hedberg 1978). These cognitive phenomena, or parts of them, have been given names such as frames of reference, myths, or strategies; here they are called organizational ideologies.

An ideology is a set of ideas. A person's ideas about one particular object or situation is here called a cognitive structure. Because people can be more or less closely related to their ideas, it is possible to distinguish three kinds of organizational ideologies. One kind is the members' individual cognitive structures. These can be called *subjective ideologies*. The members also have ideas of the cognitive structures of their colleagues. These ideas are *perceived ideologies*; what people think other people think. Finally, *objective ideologies* are ideas which are shared by all organizational members and which afford common bases for discussion and action. These different kinds of ideologies are at least partly inconsistent.

Ideologies describe both how things are and how they should be, and these two aspects are often strongly interdependent. Both the descriptive and the normative aspects answer questions about reality. One question is *how?* How do the members act in relation to each other or to people outside the organization? Another question is *what?* What has happened (history), or what will (expectations)? Ideologies define not only what is perceived as fact but also which facts appear important. Thirdly, ideologies can answer the question *why?* Causes may be attributed to an individual member, to the whole organization (self-attribution), or to the organization's environments (environmental attribution).

Organizational ideologies interrelate closely with decisions, since they make it easier for people to agree on what objectives to pursue, on what action alternatives hold promise, and on what outcomes are probable. Ideologies afford short cuts in decision-making by enabling decision-makers to omit or abbreviate some steps and by filtering out some alternatives and consequences (March and Simon 1958).

Ideologies also substitute for decisions. Many organizational actions do not follow decision processes; agreement and coordination arise without decision-making, because the actors perceive situations similarly and share expectations and general values (Danielsson and Malmberg 1979).

In the innovative company mentioned earlier, most ideas for product development projects clearly matched the ideology. Such proposals could be accepted and projects started without explicit decisions. Instead of carrying out decision-making processes, management engaged in supporting the proposals by arousing commitments and strengthening the expectations that the projects would succeed.

Organizational ideologies tend to arise by themselves in any organization, but according to some authors, they can also be consciously moulded by an organization's members (Ansoff, Declerck, and Hayes 1976; Lorange and Vancil 1977; Starbuck, Greve, and Hedberg 1978). This suggests that ideologies can be formed with the direct purpose of avoiding rational decision-making, thus reinforcing the potential for taking difficult actions. In fact, organizational ideologies might reconcile the tasks of thinking and of acting, because ideologies might identify appropriate actions and also contribute to their accomplishment.

If ideologies are to take the place of rational decision-making, confrontations between proposed actions and ideologies should give clear results. It should be possible to classify a proposal as acceptable or unacceptable after little analysis and discussion. There should be high consistency among the cognitive structures of individual organizational members. There should not only be common ideologies to undergird discussions, but these objective ideologies should be very conclusive—so clear and so narrow that additional filters for ideas are unnecessary.

Conclusiveness could be accomplished by objective ideologies that include just a few, precise normative statements. However, a confrontation between very simple ideologies and a nonconforming action proposal might throw the ideologies into question rather than the proposal. Complex ideologies that make contingent statements about an organization and its environments can also be conclusive, and such ideologies are unlikely to be challenged by a single action proposal.

A comparison between two companies revealed that the one with narrow, clear, and complex objective ideologies was able to accomplish great changes in its product mix, whereas the company with broad, ambiguous, and simple ideologies had great difficulties getting new products into production (Brunsson 1979). Ideologies which are clear, narrow, differentiated, complex, and consistent can provide good bases for action because they solve a large part of the choice problem. Such ideologies can determine what actions are right, so analysis is minimized, and efforts can concentrate on reinforcing actions. Decision rationality can be used for forming ideologies, and action rationality can be used for forming actions. Thinking can be separated from acting.

Attribution is important too. If the outcomes of action are believed to depend on environmental events, an organization should construct forecasts of the type prescribed by rational models. If the outcomes seem to depend on what members do within an organization itself, the key task is to create motivations and commitments. Thus, environmental attribution fits decision rationality, whereas self-attribution facilitates action rationality.

IDEOLOGICAL SHIFTS THAT FOSTER RADICAL CHANGES

Actions that would radically change an organization's relations to its environments are typically difficult to carry out and need strong commitments and high motivations, so ideologies should endorse these actions precisely and enthusiastically. But such ideologies constrain the possibilities for change, because only changes that match the ideologies receive ideological support.

Changes within narrow ideologies do sometimes suffice. Often, however, organizations need quick and radical changes to accommodate rapid environmental changes, and precise ideologies would rule out changes which are radical enough to cope with these situations. Yet, broad and ambiguous ideologies would not afford strong bases for action. A company which regards itself a transportation company may be no more flexible than one which considers railways its domain. There seems to be a dilemma: radical changes require conflicting qualities of organizational ideologies.

There is a solution, however. Again, the trick is to separate thinking from acting. If change actions are preceded by ideological shifts, they can attract enough support to be accomplished. This implies that change actions should wait until new ideologies have been established.

If ideologies are to serve as bases for choice, they must resist pressures for change and change slowly. In fact, the slowness of ideological shifts can explain the long time lags before organizations respond to important threats in their environments, even when the threats seem obvious to external observers (Starbuck, Greve, and Hedberg 1978).

The need for complex and precise ideologies that shift explains the 'myth cycles' reported by Jönsson and Lundin (1977). They found that organizations jump from one dominant ideology, or myth, to another. Belief in a dominant ideology is strong under normal conditions, and the dominant ideology is questioned only during crises. When members lose faith in a dominant ideology, they replace it by another. Such myth cycles imply a strong belief in one objective ideology and a consistency between subjective and objective ideologies which seem irrational from a decision-making point of view. On the other hand, the cycles contain much action rationality. A dominant ideology maximizes an organization's ability to act. Consensus and strong adherence to one ideology are not merely results of people's analytical and perceptual deficiencies; they are necessary conditions for organizational survival.

If radical changes have to be initiated by ideological shifts, it becomes a crucial issue how ideologies can be changed. External factors—such as crises or shifts in leadership—may be important, as may the properties of ideologies themselves. What properties make ideologies apt to shift when shifts are needed? Fortunately, the same properties that make ideologies good bases for action make them apt to change. Precision and complexity facilitate both.

Because descriptive statements in ideologies can be checked against reality, changes in reality provide incentives for ideological shifts. The more factors an ideology considers, the greater is the chance that some of them will change; and the more causal links among these factors, the more repercussions a change in one of them will have. If statements are clear, they can be proved false, and they have weak chances of surviving drastic changes in reality. The most stable ideologies are simple ones which are both vague and widely applicable—such as, our goal is profitability, or we shall operate in the transportation industry.

Paradoxically, the refining and elaborating of ideologies are steps towards abandoning them. However, a situation from which a change is initiated need not have much in common with the situation in which the change occurs. Existing ideologies are threatened when their implications contradict observations. If these threats cannot be met by making ideologies more ambiguous, inconsistencies arise within both subjective and objective ideologies. If subjective ideologies change more rapidly than the objective ideologies, inconsistencies arise between the two, so belief in objective ideologies decreases. Diverse subjective ideologies appear, and these may correspond to social structures different from the ones founded upon the old ideologies. The result is inconsistency between an organization's social and ideological structures, inconsistency which gives less room for compromise and authority. Differences between what people think privately and the ideologies to which they can refer publicly in their discussions give rise to misunderstandings. When people misinterpret each others' statements, conflicts arise, escalate, and remain difficult to resolve. Once the objective ideologies have been questioned, many people see chances to change the organization's environments, its internal functioning, and their own positions. The differences increase between what is and what should be, with regard to what goals to pursue, how things should be done, and who should control events.

Ideological shifts afford very bad contexts for action. Ideological inconsistencies increase uncertainty and make it extremely difficult to marshal commitments for organizational actions. Conflicts interfere with coordination. Simultaneous attempts to change environments, the ways things are done, and who has control may easily exceed an organization's problem-solving abilities. Thus, an ideological shift has to be completed before acting begins. In fact, an ideological shift in one organization produced a complete inability to act, a social deadlock where everyone worked for change, but their individual actions actually impeded change, and where no one understood how to break out of this frustrating situation (Brunsson 1981). A social deadlock is a steady state: it is full of activities, but these activities stabilize the situation, reinforcing the deadlock. A productive ideological shift must be a step in a process which leads to something new.

The difference between social deadlocks and productive ideological shifts has two implications. The first implication concerns observers of organizational changes: they might mistake confused situations for productive ideological states. Since confused situations precede the actions that create radical changes, observers might infer that confused situations produce changes, and that organizations should try to remain confused in order to have high propensities to change and high abilities to adapt to changing environments (Hedberg and Jönsson 1978). This inference neglects the transitional character of confused situations, and it mistakes processes of change for initiators of change. The confused situation during an ideological shift may resemble neither its predecessor nor its successor. On the contrary, consistent, clear, and complex ideologies are both good starting points for ideological shifts and desirable results of the shifts. Consensus rather than conflict breeds change.

The second implication is more practical: ideological shifts may become steady states. Social deadlocks are created and maintained by vicious circles in which ideological confusion leads to more confusion, and conflicts lead to still more conflicts. The confusion and conflict during an ideological shift bring an organization to the brink of social deadlock. How to prevent social deadlocks is an intriguing question for research.

CONCLUSIONS

This chapter discusses two aspects of organizations' thinking: decision-making and ideologies. Observations of organizations demonstrate that both aspects tend to be irrational in the traditional meaning of the word. Many decisions are based on biased information about a biased set of two alternatives, sometimes only one, and the information is weighed improperly. Organizational ideologies focus members' perceptions on just a few aspects of reality, and members' confidence in their biased perceptions greatly exceeds what seems justified. Organizational processes systematically reduce, rather than exploit, the multitude of perceptions that numerous people could have brought in.

These irrationalities appear both harmful and difficult to explain if the main purpose of an organization's thinking is to choose the right actions. However, the main problem for organizations is not choice but taking organized actions. Decision-making and ideologies form bases for action and can be fully understood only by recognizing that function. Thinking must be adapted to the purpose of action; and, in that perspective, irrational decision-making and narrow, prejudicial ideologies are necessary ingredients of viable organizations inhabiting complex and rough environments.

Organizations have two problems in relation to action—to find out what to do and to do it. When confronting difficult actions, organizations separate these problems. Organizations solve the problem of choice by forming ideologies, then the activities preceding specific actions focus on creating motivations and commitments.

Getting things done is particularly problematic in political organizations. These organizations institutionalize conflict: people are recruited on the basis that they adhere to disparate ideologies, and these ideological differences persist in spite of common membership in the same organizations. The ideological differences block radical actions because each proposed action is scrutinized from diverse viewpoints. Actions are supposed to be initiated by rational decision procedures that integrate the disparate viewpoints. Thus, proposed actions that involve major changes are rejected, and the organizations move in small steps (Brunsson and Jönsson 1979). Generally, political organizations try to generate action by forming strong majorities. Where this is impossible, the problems aggravate.

Lindblom (1959) argued that irrationalities can be accepted in national policy-making because policies develop incrementally. The conclusion here is instead that the high degree of rationality in political organizations produces incrementalism. It is rationality, not irrationality, that is tied to incrementalism.

Decisions and actions can also be separated organizationally. Civil servants can take actions, while the politicians discuss and debate. This heightens the chances of powerful actions but decreases the politicians' influence over what actions to take. Strong political influence seems to hinder radical changes even if there is a strong majority.

In Sweden, the control of industrial companies is shifting from managers to groups representing diverse interests, such as unions, local governments, and regional and national authorities. The industrial companies are becoming more and more like political organizations. Finding ways to combine influence by diverse groups with ability to act is a pressing challenge for organizational research.

REFERENCE

Ackerman, B. A., Ross-Ackerman, S., Sawyer, J. W., and Henderson, D. W. (1974). *The Uncertain Research for Environmental Quality*. New York: Free Press.

Ansoff, H. I., Declerck, R. P., and Hayes, R. L. (eds.) (1976). *From Strategic Planning to Strategic Management*. New York: Wiley.

Argyris, C. (1977). 'Organizational Learning and Management Information Systems', *Accounting, Organizations and Society*, 2: 113–23.

Brunsson, N. (1976). *Propensity to Change*. Goteborg, Sweden: B.A.S.

——— (1979). 'The Fallacy of Accepting Everything as a Strategy for Change', *Munich Social Science Review*, 2: 29–39.

——— (1980). 'The Functions of Project Evaluation', *R & D Management*, 10: 61–5.

——— (1981). *Politik och administration*. Stockholm: Liber.

——— and Jönsson, S. (1979). *Beslut och handling*. Falköping, Sweden: Liber.

Chandler, A. D. (1977). *The Visible Hand*. Cambridge, MA: Belknap.

Churchman, C. W. (1964). 'Managerial Acceptance of Scientific Recommendations', *California Management Review*, 7: 31–8.

Clark, B. R. (1972). 'The Organizational Saga in Higher Education', *Administrative Science Quarterly*, 17: 178–84.

Cyert, R. M. and March, J. G. (1963). *A Behavioral Theory of the Firm.* Englewood Cliffs, NJ: Prentice-Hall.

Danielsson, A. and Malmberg, A. (1979). *Beslut fattas.* Stockholm: S.A.F.

Galbraith, J. K. (1967). *The New Industrial State.* Boston, MA: Houghton Mifflin.

Goldberg, L. R. (1968). 'Simple Models or Simple Processes? Some Research on Clinical Judgments', *American Psychologist*, 23: 483–96.

Harvey, A. (1970). 'Factors Making for Implementation Success and Failure', *Management Science, Series B*, 16: 312–20.

Hedberg, B. L. T. and Jönsson, S. A. (1978). 'Designing Semi-confusing Information. Systems for Organizations in Changing Environments', *Accounting, Organizations and Society*, 3: 47–64.

Hoffman, P. J. (1968). 'Cue-consistency and Configurality in Human Judgement', in B. Kleinmetz (ed.), *Formal Representation of Human Judgement.* New York: Wiley.

Huysmans, J. H. (1970). 'The Effectiveness of the Cognitive Style Constraint in Implementing Operations Research Proposals', *Management Science*, 17: 99–103.

Janis, I. L. (1972). *Victims of Groupthink.* Boston, MA: Houghton Mifflin.

Jönsson, S. A. (1982). 'Cognitive Turning in Municipal Problem Solving', *Journal of Management Studies*, 19: 63–73.

——— and Lundin, R. A. (1977). 'Myths and Wishful Thinking as Management Tools', in P. C. Nystrom and W. H. Starbuck (eds.), *Prescriptive Models of Organizations.* Amsterdam: North-Holland, pp. 157–70.

Kahneman, D. and Tversky, A. (1973). 'On the Psychology of Prediction', *Psychological Review*, 80: 237–51.

Keeney, R. L. and Raiffa, H. (1976). *Decisions with Multiple Objectives.* New York: Wiley.

Lindblom, C. E. (1959). 'The Science of "Muddling Through" ', *Public Administration Review*, 19: 79–88.

Lindblom, C. E. (1977). *Politics and Markets.* New York: Basic Books.

Lorange, P. and Vancil, R. F. (1977). *Strategic Planning Systems.* Englewood Cliffs, NJ: Prentice-Hall.

Lundberg, E. (1961). *Produktivitet och räntabilitet.* Stockholm: S.N.S.

March, J. G. and Olsen, J. P. (eds.) (1976). *Ambiguity and Choice in Organizations.* Bergen: Universitetsforlaget.

March, J. G. and Simon, H. A. (1958). *Organizations.* New York: Wiley.

Murdick, R. G. and Ross, J. E. (1975). *Information Systems for Modern Management.* Englewood Cliffs, NJ: Prentice-Hall.

Nisbett, R. and Ross, L. (1980). *Human Inference.* Englewood Cliffs, NJ: Prentice-Hall.

Prest, A. R. and Turvey, R. (1965). 'Cost-Benefit Analysis: A Survey', *Economic Journal*, 75: 685–705.

Slovic, P. (1966). 'Cue Consistency and Cue Utilization in Judgement', *American Journal of Psychology*, 79: 427–34.

Slovic, P. (1972). *From Shakespeare to Simon*. Portland, OR: Oregon Research Institute.

Starbuck, W. H. (1976). 'Organizations and their Environments', in M. D. Dunnette (ed.), *Handbook of Industrial and Organizational Psychology*. Chicago, IL: Rand McNally, pp. 1069–123.

—— Greve, A., and Hedberg, B. L. T. (1978). 'Responding to Crises', *Journal of Business Administration*, 9(2):111–37.

Tarkowsky, Z. M. (1958). 'Symposium: Problems in Decision Taking', *Operational Research Quarterly*, 9: 121–3.

Tversky, A. and Kahneman, D. (1974). 'Judgement Under Uncertainty: Heuristics and Biases', *Science*, 185: 1124–31.

Zander, A. (1971). *Motives and Goals in Groups*. New York: Academic Press.

4

Implementing Reforms*

One February day in 1987, the board of directors of Swedish Rail (Statens Järnvägar, SJ) met to consider a plan drawn up by an international consultancy company. The idea was to implement a radical reform, the 'New SJ'. In spite of a series of earlier attempts at reform, SJ was again going through some lean years with stagnating traffic and heavy losses. Both SJ's management and its owners, represented by the Swedish Ministry of Transport, were anxious to implement rapid changes for the better. The consultancy company had been called in to think out these changes and help to carry them through. The basic idea was to make the company more businesslike. SJ was to be run as a company and not as a government service, and its corporate aim was to be a profitable business. SJ was to become the best transport company in the world and one of the most attractive workplaces in Sweden. According to the consultants' plans, this was to be achieved through 'market orientation, adaptation of resources, and decentralization' including concentration on rail traffic, improved financial control, and decentralized responsibility for results. The building and maintenance of the track infrastructure was to be separated from SJ through the creation of a state agency, the Swedish Rail Administration. SJ was to concentrate on the main business concept, running a railway service.

This was not the first time SJ had been subjected to attempts at radical reform (Brunsson, Forssell, and Winberg 1989), and the content of previous reforms had not been all that different from the one now proposed. Reforms of SJ's organization had been considered or attempted at roughly five- to ten-year intervals since the organization was founded in 1869. Much of the core content of the New SJ had also been an important part of earlier reforms. The need to be more businesslike and market oriented had been proclaimed in most reforms since 1893, including the latest one, VO 80, which had been carried out between 1979 and 1982. Ever since 1906, voices had been raised in favour of improving the company's business profile by having representatives of Swedish trade and industry on the board. The question of decentralization contracentralization had been discussed in all the previous reform programmes; the majority of the past reformers, like the reformers

---

* This chapter was co-authored by Hans Winberg

promoting the New SJ, considered decentralization a necessity. Decentralized responsibility for results was the main idea behind VO 80. The idea of separating the business side from the rail administration, forming one company-like organization and one state agency, represented a return to the organization used prior to 1888.

It is natural to ask why the reformers promoting the New SJ proposed solutions which had already been tried several times and failed. One reason might be (and was) the supply of forgetfulness. Another reason might have been that, although attempts had been made in earlier reform programmes to implement the same solutions, these attempts had not completely succeeded, and this made it seem necessary to try again. The general consensus about VO 80 was that it had never been implemented. SJ's history of reforms shows that it does not appear difficult to launch reforms, but that it is far more difficult to implement them. This chapter addresses the question of why reforms may be difficult to implement. We suggest that there are certain fundamental and common characteristics of administrative reforms which make them difficult to implement by nature, taking the implementation of the New SJ as our example.

THE NEW SJ

As it was presented in February 1987, the proposal for the New SJ reform was described in very general terms. It presented the ideas in principle, while leaving all the rest to those who were to formulate the more specific programmes; this was a deliberate strategy. The aim was to try to change the SJ culture, or people's ways of thinking, making more space for creativity and new ideas. The reformers thought that this would also make the employees behave differently and that the organization's performance would improve. The major internal changes would be prepared and effected through special projects. Market orientation in the organization would be increased through a change in attitude, with all employees learning to put business and profit first. There would be more efficient utilization of capital, and operations would be rationalized. To facilitate this, a decentralized and more flexible business organization was to be constructed.

Responsibility for both results and production would be delegated. This would be done by drawing up a new system for financial control, and by developing new procedures for planning, coordination, and scheduling of trains, making the products the basis of operations. Each train would be seen as a product and a profit centre. Personnel with product responsibility would schedule and coordinate the trains on this basis. Finally, the whole corporate group would concentrate its operations on running the railway, selling off other operations.

In the autumn of 1988, it was declared that the New SJ had been implemented. However, it had had no major impact on behaviour in the organization. Many people at the operational level still did not know of the reform or did not know that it had been implemented. A new organizational chart was introduced, according to which the old matrix organization was replaced with a divisional organization, the number of market regions was reduced, and they were renamed 'business areas'. But no new control system was developed, nor was the scheduling and coordination of the trains decentralized. The idea of working out profits in terms of train units was abandoned, and the planning of train services remained centralized. The idea of limiting the group's activities to running the railway also disappeared with the accession of a new management which decided to retain profitable activities outside the railway area as well. And the year after the reform was implemented, SJ continued to operate at a loss.

What the reform did have was a considerable effect on the company's relations with its environment. When the Swedish Rail Administration was separated from SJ, a cost of 600 million kronor (£60 million) was removed from the group. The state gave SJ better working conditions: it was freer and more like a business enterprise. Last but not least, SJ succeeded in recruiting a new board and a new management, both with greater competence in doing business.

In the remainder of this chapter we use the New SJ as an example to discuss some problems of reform implementation. We examine the discrepancy between the simplicity of reforms and the complexity of reality. We describe how reform work can be organized in a way that isolates reform ideas from practice and vice versa, and how the time lag between the formulation of ideas and implementation means that a reform's ideas go on being developed, and new reforms launched, until it ultimately becomes unclear which ideas are actually meant to be implemented.

THE SIMPLICITY OF REFORMS AND THE COMPLEXITY OF REALITY

The most striking characteristic of the ideas launched in the New SJ was their simplicity. This was in contrast to most people's ideas about the present situation, which were characterized by complexity. Railway operations may appear to be extremely complex, and many people at SJ saw its operations that way. There are close technical links between what the various units do: at any point in time there are thousands of engines and carriages in hundreds of terminals or on different parts of the railway network, and their locations at that point in time determine what can be done next. Customers use thousands of different combinations of routes along the lines for their trips or for transportation of goods; less busy lines feed into busier ones which feed back into less busy ones again. Transport sold in one region gives rise to costs in others.

One important tool for handling this complexity was the annual train plan drawn up by the train planning department in an effort to optimize capital use. Train timetables were determined by this plan. For example, the plan scheduled extremely complex routes for engines: an engine might be on the move for weeks without returning to the station from which it departed. In addition to all this complexity, there was the complexity of the previous business concept, according to which SJ was both a business enterprise and a state agency: it was supposed both to be a profit-making business and to satisfy political requirements. All this complexity had led, among other things, to a number of different regional and functional organizational charts being tried over a century of reforms.

Simplification by Reform

In contrast to the existing complexity, the New SJ offered many kinds of sim-plification. One basic simplification was that the company was to be coupled to only one of the two institutions of business enterprise and state agency. It was to be a business enterprise, and not subject to special political require-ments. Another simplification was the idea that dealing with the railway tracks was to be separated and assigned to the Swedish Rail Administration. The reformers also wanted to make a clear distinction, in terms of personnel and accounting, between the passenger traffic division and the freight traffic division. As mentioned, operations not clearly related to rail traffic were to be sold off. When negotiating financing with the state, SJ had, for years, used highly simplified models of the railway network, divided into profitable and unprofitable lines. This idea of distinguishing between different lines was used in the New SJ to provide a foundation for structuring the organization. Each line was to be seen as a profit unit, for which a regional group was responsible. The reformers had the idea that the various regional groups would 'own' not only the individual lines, but also the rolling stock on their parts of the line. The regional groups were also to be further subdivided into even smaller profit centres. The idea was to decentralize profit responsibility as far as possible in the organization; when it came to passenger traffic this meant down to the level of each individual train.

This simplicity was contrasted with the prevailing situation, where both operations and the picture of them were complex. For instance, the accounting system reflected this complexity, which made it impossible to measure profits further down than at director general level. The simplicity also contrasted with people's general conception of the previous reform. VO 80 was seen as having led to far too complex ideas, for example the idea of the matrix organization.

However, not all the simplifications in the New SJ actually held up to implementation. It became apparent, for example, that the delegation of responsibility for material and personnel down to unit levels would lead to a far greater need for materials than under the old system. The idea of making each individual train a profit unit was also abandoned. Profitable operations unrelated to the railway were retained.

Thus simplifying ideas did not result in corresponding simplifications in action. But by the time that was clear, the simplicity of the ideas had probably accomplished their task. This type of simplification strategy is common in conjunction with reforms. Reforms are attempts to organize afresh, to give organizations new forms. When, or for as long as, reforms are ideological, they take place in thoughts, not in action or in material operations. It is a matter of constructing the organization in one's head, of organizing an image. In some respects there is greater freedom in the world of ideas than in the world of action. Many material restrictions can be neglected. This makes it possible to organize one's picture according to the principle of simplicity, despite the complexities of reality. So reformers have the freedom to simplify, but it can also be argued that there is good reason for them to make use of this freedom.

One argument is that simplification is an attempt to gain control. Having control of something tangible means being able to govern it; having control over an existing organization means being able to steer it in the desired direction. It is often very difficult to exercise this control, and this is an important reason for proposing reforms, reforms that will change an organization so as to make it more governable. And one main cause of a lack of control is exactly that the complexity is too great, that is so great that control also becomes far too complex, or so great that it becomes impossible to see how governance might even be carried out, what strings to pull to direct the organization. The essence of the concept of 'organizing' may even be said to be reduction of complexity. And thus simplifying reality in accordance with a simplified picture offers the hope of future control. We might say that reforms which simplify are aimed at changing organizations so they become easier to govern, and consequently easier to reform, in the future.

Another related reason for reformers' interest in simplification is the need for understanding. It is difficult to understand complex organizations and how they function. Reformers have the advantage of being able to change organizations, and strictly speaking all they need is to understand the new organization. The new organization only exists in their own minds: what they have to understand is their own image of the organization, and the simpler the picture is, the easier that will be. It is also easier to communicate a simple picture and make it comprehensible to others.

The substantial simplification of the ideas in the New SJ was facilitated by two of their other characteristics: their vagueness and their being rooted in a familiar institution. Although the ideas were simple and clear, they were not particularly precise. The most precise definition of being businesslike was 'more in than out'. Although it was quite clear what this meant on a general level, what it would imply for action was not specified from the outset. The principle was clear, its impact was not spelled out. Vagueness is the term we use to describe such clear principles with ambiguous consequences. Vagueness was an important way of keeping the ideas simple: possible criticism that they were too simple or too general could easily be met by saying that they would be developed and specified in closer contact with the specific SJ reality.

As the ideas were part of a familiar institution (the business enterprise), and since market orientation and decentralization were in fashion at the moment, it was easy (rightly or wrongly) to get the impression that the same principles had been successfully applied in other organizations. This made it difficult to see why the ideas would not work in the context of SJ. There was no reason to demand information immediately about what was really meant. In addition, an institution such as the business enterprise consists of a package of ideas and requires consideration of the whole package, not individual details in it. The question was whether to accept the general idea of becoming a true business enterprise. 'I believe in the entirety', was how one leading reformer expressed it.

Vagueness and institutional links, combined with simplicity, also made it easier for the reformers and those around them to establish a firm conviction that the reform was right. Vagueness enabled some wishful thinking and optimism about the potential for good detailed solutions in the future. Since the principles were derived from a well-known institution they had a semblance of general good sense. It seemed unnecessary to consider other alternative reforms or to forecast the consequences of the reforms in any detail at an early stage. Moreover, what was being held up for comparison was the current management strategy, which was strikingly inconsistent, unclear, and incapable of achieving satisfactory results. Presenting more alternatives or detailed impact assessments might have created uncertainty as to whether the reform was a good one or the best possible one, or whether the reform was really going to be implemented, and this might threaten its support base. Avoiding detailed analysis reduces uncertainty and facilitates action; it is an expression of 'action rationality' (Brunsson 1985).

There was such firm conviction that it was even possible to officially state how much the reform was expected to yield in financial terms—1,000 million kronor (£100 million)—without analysing how this was to be achieved. There was less certainty about this sum in private conversation, but people still considered it obvious that the reform should have the proposed content. Action rationality was also an expressed policy of the consultancy firm: their main idea was to invest in what they called rapid implementation rather than in long analyses.

Action rationality meant that the reform projects were easily and rapidly initiated. However, it proved more difficult to implement the reform ideas in practice. Their simplicity and vagueness made the ideas useless or difficult to use in the complex production process. Many of the people who worked with the day-to-day running of SJ's activities complained that they were not given any information: they did not realize there was no meaningful information to be given. Management and the reformers issued a great deal of information which was meaningful to themselves, but not to other people in the organization.

In conclusion, the New SJ exemplifies how administrative reforms are facilitated because they are about the future. Since reforms concern the future, they can long be maintained at the level of ideas, where it is possible to accomplish greater and more clearly positive things than can normally be achieved in practice. Thus they easily gain the support of many, and this support results in their being initiated. However, the same simplicity which acquires support also creates difficulties in implementation. Simplicity and complexity pose a dilemma for reformers: simple reforms gain support easily, but are difficult to implement, while reforms complex enough to reflect reality are more suited to being carried out, but more difficult to secure support for.

Separating Ideas and Practice

A project organization was created to implement the New SJ. The idea was to use a number of projects to investigate how the ideas were to be transformed into practice, and also to initiate their implementation. The project groups represented a sort of new organization parallel to the ordinary one. The terms and conditions applying to the project work differed from those applying to ordinary operations, as they were related to the world of ideas and were concerned with the future, and thus were able to neglect the prevailing complex reality. The project groups were partly composed of SJ employees and partly of consultants. The project members identified strongly with their roles in the reform work. They saw their roles as being quite different from that of operative personnel. In earlier reforms, many of these had been in operative positions themselves: 'I was on a different level then, so I didn't really notice the reforms' was a typical statement. Only project members or leaders were considered to be working with reforms.

The temporary organization created in this way meant that ordinary operations were decoupled from the ideas. The project members worked with ideas. Their mission was to articulate ideas for future practices, to distinguish them from prevailing practices, and thus to endow future operations with meaning. In the project, it seemed to be not only meaningful but also vital to work in abstract: the ideas had to be reformulated and left to mature before they could influence the practices of the future. Meanwhile, the operative personnel worked according to their daily routines and 'did as we'd always done'. They could easily proceed with their old routines, since no one was asking them to make their present work meaningful: since a reform was being worked out, things were certain to change soon, and for the better. It was not necessary to justify present operations by connecting them to good ideas, so present actions and actors were not disturbed by lofty ideas and ideologies.

So the ideas were liberated from the complex operations which, in turn, were liberated from the abstract ideas, so difficult to associate with daily routines. The isolation between the reform project and operations made it possible to keep ideas on the agenda which would otherwise have been seen as impossible, and hence abandoned. The isolation also made it possible to use the reform organization as a buffer in time between ideas and practices, since the projects took, and were intended to take, time. Reforms must necessarily take time if the project members are to implement their work. This lag in time complicates the implementation of reforms considerably, as the next section elucidates.

The Difficult Time

Launching a reform is like making a decision. At a given time, the people whose ideas are expected to be implemented in practice announce which ideas are to be carried out. They commit themselves and others to ideas they have at the moment of launching the reform or making the decision. Ideas are constantly evolving, but in order to endow the operation with some backbone, certain ideas must be held static, at least for some time. Often, such ideas are put on paper, where they do not change. But it is difficult for reformers and decision-makers to decide to stop thinking, and so there is always the 'risk' that they will develop newer, better, or more thought-through ideas, and thereby come to consider their old ideas as bad. And of course this risk increases over time. As mentioned above, during the first year of the New SJ, project groups worked with the aim of making each moving train, that is each departure, a separate profit unit. During the course of the project, this was changed to apply to each individual stretch of railway line. When the new management was appointed, this profit-centre idea was altered again, as it was considered unnecessary to measure the results for such small units. Consequently, during the two years of project work, no system of profit-centre measurement at these levels was established.

Ideas also change as a result of the reactions they provoke, both inside and outside the organization, when they are presented. One example of how ideas develop as a result of outside reactions was the idea of the business enterprise. When the initial thinking about the New SJ reform took shape and was approved by management and the owners' representatives, there was a strong belief that SJ should be given the same terms as any business enterprise. All parties considered this necessary if it were to be possible to run SJ as such. The old idea of making the former public utility into a joint-stock company was relaunched; but it was rejected internally at a relatively early stage since it was considered unrealistic. It was reformulated in terms of far-reaching and specific demands for financial independence and discretion, albeit within the confines of the public utility. Reactions from the owners and other groups, not least the trade unions, however, made it necessary to modify these demands, and less far-reaching changes were accepted. One example was the size of investment decisions which SJ could make itself, where the compromise agreed upon was 20 million kronor (£2 million), instead of an unlimited sum.

Operative personnel also reacted to the proposed ideas for change. The project members sometimes had to look for support from operative personnel in formulating specific action plans. When that happened, the ideas were sometimes changed radically in the process, and sometimes even rejected altogether; albeit only occasionally, since ideas about change were often so general and future oriented that they left room for many conclusions. Another way in which ideas were changed was when people in the organization were replaced, for instance when the new director was appointed. New people also reacted to the reform ideas.

The first situation, when the operative personnel reacted, was experienced in relation to the train plan project. Originally, the reformers and project members had intended the entire train planning work, that is work with plans for directing all traffic on the railways, to be decentralized. In their opinion, the train plan had come to govern all the work too much, and had come to stand as an obstacle to flexibility. However, there was such strong resistance to the decentralization of this planning work that nothing radical was actually done in the new organizational structure. It was said that more information was to be sent from local officials responsible for products, and that there would be shorter time lags between the original impulse and a change in the timetable, but there was no real decentralization.

There were two changes of management during the course of the reform, and this meant that the ideas changed. The information function provides a clear example of how signals were altered rapidly and radically. The original idea was to delegate responsibility for information throughout the organization. In order to ensure that all employees could be reached when necessary, people were to learn to take more independent initiatives and sometimes cut across the traditional hierarchy. The new management reversed this strategy, and held to the opinion that information needed to be uniform, and that it should therefore always emanate from the central information staff.

New Reforms

Another difficulty in implementing reforms is that they sometimes give rise to new reforms even before they have been implemented. New reforms either can result from slowness in implementing the old ones, or it may take time to implement the old ones because ideas for new ones come up, or both conditions may apply. VO 80 had not been completed when the New SJ was launched, nor was the New SJ completely implemented before new reforms were launched. But in both cases the reform work was declared complete by the management as soon as the new organizational structure had been introduced.

One of the reforms after the New SJ consisted of a new method of strategic planning which, with respect to its simplicity, was extremely reminiscent of the early versions of the New SJ. Another was the establishment of new business plans for the various divisions, where it was specified what was to be accomplished, rather than how things were to be organized. The business plans stated objectives and how they were to be achieved, for instance which groups of customers to invest in and how to adapt products to suit them. VO 80 was seen by many people to be too complex and therefore not sufficiently attractive. Management complained that it was difficult for them to put across the message of VO 80. For this reason, they hired the consultants, but they reached the conclusion that there was nothing wrong with the information; rather a new reform was needed. Thus management's attempt to better implement the old reform led to a new one.

Similarly, the New SJ led to the recruitment of new management, and this new management naturally had ideas that were somewhat different from those of the consultants. Implementation of the new organization had, furthermore, been delayed, and if profitability were to be achieved it was high time to start taking measures in practice; there was no time to wait until the new organization was ready. Interest in the new organization faded rapidly, and management finally announced that the new organization was now implemented. Nothing much remained of the forceful slogans from the New SJ's initial launch about all the positive effects the new organization would have. The announcement that the reform could be considered complete also suggests that the management wished to wash its hands of responsibility for the more complex ideas of the later stages of the reform. And the reform no longer offered improved understanding.

PRESENTATION AND RESULTS

The New SJ was presented like many other reforms. Three ways in which it was described were particularly important. First, it was presented as a way of changing the organization itself: the audience was the SJ employees, they were the ones who were supposed to listen to the reformers and then change their behaviour. Second, the ultimate aim of the reform was presented as being to change operations at the technological core of the organization, to change its ways of producing and selling transport. Finally, the effects of the reform were presented as being in the future. A great deal of work in 'implementing' the reform, of organizing things differently and of getting people to change their behaviour, remained to be done. The reformers said that the effects of the reforms would not be apparent for five to ten years. It is difficult to say what the reformers' innermost intentions were, but we gained the impression that the way they presented the reform reflected their own objectives and convictions. Seemingly they both wanted the effects to be these and believed that they would be.

All these ways of presenting the reform proved to be at odds with how it worked in practice. The reform did have an internal audience, but the effects on the external audience proved much more important. The major changes brought about by the reform—including the new rules for relations with the state, the division into a business enterprise and the Swedish Rail Administration, writing off of capital, and recruitment of a new board and management—were all effects of changes in attitude and behaviour in persons outside the organization.

Although the reformers spoke a great deal about operations, they mostly worked with ideology and structure, with describing how people should think and which organizational structures would be useful. They did not devote themselves to changing the products, but to changing what they thought of as the structural and ideological prerequisites for the products to change.

The future effects of the New SJ were what the reformers talked about, but these were very uncertain, particularly as the reform was soon said to be complete and was replaced with new ideas. The New SJ reform was declared complete when many employees in the organization had not received any concrete information about what the reform was going to involve, what changes would affect them, or what demands for changes in behaviour were being placed on them. It is hard to see that their future actions would be affected.

So instead of affecting future internal operations, the reform had fairly dramatic effects on SJ's external relations and its management's work while the reform was in progress. Rather than changing products and production the reform influenced external parties' ideas about SJ, and it forced management to work with ideological issues rather than with production.

One interpretation of the difference between the presentation and the results is that the New SJ failed: it did not achieve, and could not reasonably have been expected to achieve, what the reformers had promised. But another interpretation is that the reform was extremely successful, albeit not in the manner that had been predicted. The reform had major ideological external effects at the time it was ongoing, and if reforms generally have their greatest effects at the start of their existence, when they are sold to the organization and initiated, it may be a good thing if they later fail according to their own criteria: if they are seen as failing, this may give rise to arguments for new reforms which in turn quickly produce new effects.

The objectives stated by the reformers may not always be followed by the desired results; good objectives may have other effects. Precisely because SJ's production and results still did not improve, it was important to disseminate the hope that production and results would improve: interested parties both inside and outside the company would then be willing to wait for the future effects. The important effect of the reform was not improved operations, but the hope of improved operations. And to spread this hope the reform had to be presented as aiming at improved operations.

IMPLEMENTING REFORMS: A MODEL

The case of the New SJ presents a series of complications and difficulties both when it comes to implementing reforms and to defining what are good ways of implementing them, and even in generally defining implementation. In this final section we summarize the discussion with a simple model of implementation, which can deal with some complications.

Time as a Complication

Implementation can be defined as a process by which reformers' ideas are put into practice. If the reformers' ideas control and permeate operations in the organization, the reform is implemented, that is there is consistency between idea and practice. Our study of the New SJ, however, demonstrates that this model for implementation is too simple and needs to be made somewhat more complex in order to be realistic. What distinguishes reforms is that it takes some time to implement them; ideas are not transformed into practice immediately. This is why we talk about a specific implementation process.

If the reformers' ideas remain stable over time, the delay between ideas and new practice does not represent a problem for our definitions of implementation and implemented. But if the reformers' ideas change over time the model becomes more complicated. Which ideas should characterize practices, the ones the reformers have when the reform commences or the ones they have when the reform is completed? If implementation means that the original ideas govern practice, even when the reformers' ideas have changed, it also means that the reformers are doomed to feel dissatisfied in a world where their reforms are implemented; neither at the start of the reforms nor at their conclusion will practices be consistent with the reformers' ideas. This implies that the implementation of reforms does not do away with the tension between idea and practice which gives rise to reforms, rather that its existence is upheld. If, instead, implementation is taken to have occurred when the reformees behave as the reformers want them to at that same point in time, the implementation process must be characterized by the reformees not having adapted to the ideas presented by the reformers when they launched the reforms. If reformers' ideas develop over time, implementation cannot possibly both mean that the original reform ideas control practice and that the reformers are content.

As we have tried to illustrate with the case of the New SJ, there are many reasons to expect that reformers' ideas do develop over time. Announcing an idea for reform can be seen as an attempt to stop thinking, to 'decide' that these ideas will prevail for some future period. But ideas are so easy to reshape and renew that it may be difficult for the reformers themselves to abide by their decision. Nor does it seem to be particularly intelligent to stop thinking, or to become as slow at thinking as the organization is slow at moving.

In the New SJ, we saw that one reason for ideas developing was that reforms led to new reforms long before they had been implemented. Ideas easily give rise to new ideas, without the first ideas being tested in practice. Experimenting is not the only way to learn. If we think we are wrong, there is good reason to think again before it is too late, rather than waiting for the practical results of each new thought.

The reform ideas may also be changed quite simply by the reformers' disappearance, because the people who launched a reform are replaced by new people and therefore do not evaluate it. This may sometimes happen quite shortly after the reform has been launched. This is a typical course of events when professional reformers, such as consultants, are called in. They are experts in launching reforms rather than implementing them. In the case of SJ, one important result of the reform was that the management was replaced and that the new management hired new consultants.

If the implementation process contains the complications described here, this will affect how implementation is achieved. It will be impossible to both implement the original ideas of the reform and to ensure that practice at a certain point in time corresponds with the reformers' ideas. If reformees want to invest in the first alternative, implementation of the original intentions of the reform, they should register the ideas in detail and then try to implement them without having any contact with the reformers; contact with the reformers' new ideas may confuse them. If this rule is followed, the reforms will be implemented more easily, but implementation means that the reformers will not be satisfied.

If reformees want to carry through the second alternative, there are several strategies they can adopt. The most fundamental thing for them is not to follow the ideas presented by the reformers when they launch the reform. This slightly increases the chances that some of the reformers' ideas will correspond with practice when the reform has been implemented. Reformers sometimes complain that it is difficult and lengthy to persuade the reformees to change their behaviour in practice according to the reformers' desires. But as demonstrated here, this type of resistance seems sensible even from the reformers' point of view since it increases their chances of experiencing the reform as successful.

In order to further increase the chances of implementation according to the second definition, the reformees could try to predict the reformers' future ideas and develop their practices in line with their predictions, that is the ideas to which they suppose the present thoughts of the reformers will lead. In order to do this, the reformees need to be able to think as strategically as the reformers.

The most effective means of achieving consistency between the reformers' ideas and practice is for the reformees to control the reformers instead of the other way round. If the reformees can convince the reformers that the right ideas are the ones reflected in current practice, then ideas and practice will correspond. Practice will be implemented in the world of ideas rather than vice versa. The reason for this being a more effective implementation strategy is quite simply the difference in the speed of adaptation between ideas and practice we have assumed. If ideas can be adapted to practice momentarily, or at very short notice, but not the other way round, consistency will, of course, most easily be reached through changing the ideas. The most satisfied reformers are those who launch reforms which describe the present and unchanging state of practices or the state in which practices are inevitably moving; such reforms create ideologies about, explain, and justify what is being done in practice, or what those in operative positions want to do.

The assumed difference in speed between the development of ideas and the development of practices may also have another effect on the content of reforms. It may be tempting for reformers to try reforming things that can be changed quickly, for example redrawing an organizational chart rather than changing attitudes, installing ready-made, standardized accounting systems rather than developing systems of their own, even if the latter would have a better chance of affecting behaviour within their organization. It may also be tempting to launch ideas which can be assumed to be more stable than others. Ideas which are parts of institutions, for instance ideas which relate to traditional, accepted thinking about what a company is, may be assumed to be more enduring than the reformers' own innovations and therefore more attractive. And some reformers might expect their more abstract desires, such as making the organization more like a business enterprise, to last longer than more detailed ideas on how these desires should be put into practice, for instance ideas for a new budgeting system.

Ambiguity and Implementation

We have assumed up to this point that it is easy to decide what the reformers' ideas are and what things look like in practice. Let us now add another complication, ambiguity. At the time when the reforms are considered to have been implemented it may not be clear what the reformers' original ideas really were; the ideas may have been ambiguous ever since the reforms were launched or they may be unclear because time has passed. Decisions about reforms are sometimes ambiguous, for instance when they are the result of compromises (Baier, March, and Saetren 1986) or when reform ideas are vague, as in the

New SJ. This type of ambiguity can be exploited for retrospective rationalization: when the reforms are considered to have been implemented, the original ideas for reform are interpreted and presented so as to match practice at that point in time.

What goes on in practice may also be ambiguous; it may be difficult to know what is really happening and how to describe it (Sahlin-Andersson 1989), and this makes it difficult to decide whether it matches the reform ideas or not. It may be particularly difficult for the reformers, who are at a certain distance from practice, to decide this. Reformees who want to satisfy reformers can choose to respond to the reformers' ideology with repeating the same ideology and to describe practices so that they seem to correspond to the reformers' ideas.

Ambiguity about the original ideas of the reform is the most forceful kind of ambiguity. It may efface difficulties that the earlier complications gave rise to. In other words, ambiguity may contribute to implementation in both the senses we have referred to: practice may appear to correspond both to the earlier ideas of the reform and the current ones, since they appear to be the same.

Reforming the Environment

Finally, let us introduce a further complication into our model. Up until now, the model has described two parties, the reformers and the reformees. But if we are to believe many reformers, including those at SJ, these are not the only relevant parties. The reformers want to change the reformees, but the ultimate purpose of doing so is often to improve the organization's relationship with its environment. SJ was to become more like a business enterprise in order to make more money in its contacts with customers, the financial sector, the government, and other important groups in the world around the organization. Thus the environments of the reformers and the reformees are expected to react to the modified practices of the reformees.

If the ultimate purpose of the reformers in advocating a particular reform is to influence the organization's environment, the definition of implementation as changes in practice is too limited. Instead, a reform has really only been implemented when it has impacted on the environment.

Effects on the environment can be the result of changes in practice, but they can also occur as a direct result of the reformers presenting their ideas. When people outside the organization listen to the talk of the reformers, they may believe that practices are going to change, and already begin to adapt themselves, in relation to their picture of future practices. But they may also feel that the reformers' ideas are important in themselves, for example that they correspond better with their own views of how an organization should be controlled and function. In the case of SJ, we have seen that the reformers' ideas had a direct impact on the financiers and on recruitment on top managers, and this meant better business.

If the ultimate effects of the reforms are to be on outsiders' views of the organization, the problems we have discussed with regard to implementation and time delays disappear, or at least diminish. In principle, there is nothing to prevent ideas about the organization that are current in the environment from changing as rapidly as the reformers' ideas. In order to be satisfied with the results, reformers simply have to adhere to their ideas for as long as it takes to convince the environment of them.

Of course, the reformers may have higher ambitions than only to influence the opinions of the environment. They may also want these new opinions held by outside interests to influence those people's actions. The same problem may then arise in the external interests' organizations as in the reformers': it may take time to change practices. However, within the company, the reformers want administrative changes that often take a long time to implement, but the changes in the environment's practices they want to achieve may materialize more quickly—as the New SJ again exemplifies. At SJ, the reformers wanted to achieve complicated organizational and behavioural changes within the organization, but when it came to external interests, they simply wanted to see more money come into the company, and they wanted competent personnel to apply for employment with SJ. These last two changes were changes which could, and did, take place rapidly. By changing external interests' view of the company, SJ rapidly gained more money and a highly qualified management.

When reformers strive to influence the organization's environment directly through reform ideas, and not through the practices of the reformees, they have less reason to be interested in these practices. The practices can then develop in their own way, separate from the reformers' ideas. And the reformers can develop their ideas, separate from organizational practice. This gives a completely different mechanism for reforming than the difference between ideas and practice. Reformers can be expected to launch reforms irrespective of what the current practices are. Reforms become attempts to influence outsiders via ideas, and as soon as outside interest in the organization cools off, or its values about what the organization should be change, it is time to launch a new reform. Whether or not earlier reforms have been implemented in internal practice makes no difference. The reformers' satisfaction or dissatisfaction, and their reforms, are independent of whether or not their ideas are consistent with practices in the organization. Also, the content of reform becomes independent of the content of current practice. A reform may contain suggestions for new ways in which practice can function, or it could just as well have the same content as present practice. The reformers may propose a practice that is already in place, since they are unaware of current practice; or sometimes even for the very reason that they are aware of it and think it is consistent with outsiders' views of how organizations should work. People at the operational level in large organizations will recognize this type of reform.

Implementation Strategies

We have argued that implementation of reforms in practice may encounter a number of complications. The complications we have discussed are that reforms take time to implement, reformers' ideas are not stable, there may be a difference in pace between the development of ideas and the development of practices, ideas and practices are ambiguous, and the reactions of the environment are more important than the reactions of the organization. Given these complications, there are four main ways of implementing reforms. From a normative point of view, they all have pros and cons.

The first type of implementation—implementing the reformers' original ideas—creates both dissatisfaction and a good starting point for new reforms, which in turn may create even more reforms. What we think of this result will depend on how we value reforms. Reforms may represent development, the desire for improvement, and a struggle for higher values than we normally achieve in our daily activities; but reforms can also been seen as unrealistic projects and a waste of resources.

The second implementation strategy is that the reformees try to guess what the reformers' future ideas will be, and try to adapt to them. This seems to be a completely sensible method, but only if we ignore the uncertainty of those guesses.

The third implementation strategy is to adapt ideas to practice, which can be simplified by, but does not presuppose, ambiguity in ideas and practice. This strategy is more prone to create satisfaction and the peace and quiet required to get work done. But adapting ideas to practice may squeeze the goodness, justice, and beauty common in reform ideas out of the picture. This development is seen in many contexts to be morally dubious: good morality presupposes the existence of sin, of peoples' values being so grand that they are unable to translate them into action. This method of implementation may also inhibit the intellect, making people think more slowly than is necessary.

The final strategy is to isolate reforms from operations, by, for example, reforming the environment rather than the organization itself. This type of isolation preserves beautiful ideas and the right to go on thinking. However, these effects are achieved not by people constantly striving for new goals in action but by creating the illusion of always treading the path of virtue. This may be a pleasant illusion, but it is also too close to hubris not to give rise to moral complications.

REFERENCES

Baier, V. E., March, J. G., and Saetren, H. (1986). 'Implementation and Ambiguity', *Scandinavian Journal of Management Studies*, 2(3–4): 197–212.

Brunsson, N. (1985). *The Irrational, Organization: Irrationality as a Basis for Organizational Action and Change*. Chichester, UK: Wiley.

—— Forssell, A., and Winberg, H. (1989). *Reform som tradition*. Stockholm: EFI.

Sahlin-Andersson, K. (1989). *Oklarhetens strategi*. Lund, Sweden: Studentlitteratur.

5

Responsibility as an Impediment to Influence—The Case of Budgeting

In the present chapter I demonstrate that decision-makers may be more interested in the responsibility effects of their decisions than in the decision content, one reason being that there may be a connection between responsibility and influence: the assumption of responsibility can mean a loss of influence. An organizational management can increase its influence by avoiding decisions and the responsibility that goes with them. It is this relationship which will be exemplified in the following description of a common type of decision process, namely budgeting.

BUDGETING

Budgeting is a common form of decision process in organizations. Like many other organizational techniques it stems originally from the public sector. The importance of budgeting in this sector depends partly on the fact that a good deal of the funds available for distribution are derived from taxes and are thus independent of the production of individual goods or services. This means that the money is usually collected in a central unit, which then has to distribute it to various production units before production can occur. This type of redistribution problem does not necessarily arise in organizations where the production units acquire money direct from sales. However, this has not stopped the rapid spread of the budgeting technique over the last twenty years or so, even in organizations—private and public—which do acquire their revenues in this way.

But budgeting need not be concerned exclusively with the solution of a technical redistribution problem; the budgeting processes may have other causes and effects. The great importance of budgeting in the public sector suggests that it may have a role in politics: 'Budgeting lies at the heart of the policy process', as Wildavsky (1975) put it after studying national budgeting in a number of countries. In a study of municipal budgeting Olsen (1971) found that the budget process mainly fulfilled a symbolical function. In normative budgeting theory and in Wildavsky (1974, 1975) the budget seems to be regarded as an important instrument of control in organizations. As we see in the following discussion, the budget process can fulfil all these functions.

The budget is a decision on a grand scale: on one single occasion the organizational leadership makes decisions about virtually all operations over a future period, generally the coming year. The link between decisions and operations consists of money: the content of the decisions is the promise of money to various units or programmes. Instructions of a more or less concrete nature about the activities for which the money is to be used can be attached to the decisions. But compared with the type of decisions discussed in the last chapter, the coupling between budget decisions and action is a very loose one.

Budgeting and Hypocrisy

Because of its relatively loose links with action, budgeting provides a good instrument for conducting politics and producing hypocrisy. Inconsistencies can easily arise between the budget decisions and the action performed during the year. The fact that money has been allocated to an operation does not necessarily mean that the operation will take place; obstacles may well appear. Up to a point the inconsistencies can be regulated, depending on how much weight is given to budget control. If no great effort is made to check how the money is being used, or very little store is set by this kind of budget control, then inconsistencies are more likely to arise. If inconsistencies are discovered and criticized, the criticism can be dismissed on the grounds that management has done what it could by making the money available, and that it is the operational side which has failed to use it, or has wasted it, or has used it for something else—all of which can be blamed on operational incompetence or contrariness.

The budget is a plan concerning the future. It therefore also provides excellent opportunities for hypocrisy in the form of discrepancies between present and past behaviour and promises for the future. The budget also offers a good opportunity to produce talk and decisions along the lines that 'everything will be better in the future', particularly if the past or the present leave little to boast about. Many organizations appear to be much more interested in discussing their budgets than analysing their accounts (Brorström 1982, 1985). They often base their new budget on the figures in the previous one rather than on any accounting data; figures for current or even the previous year are not usually available when the new budget is being prepared. This often leads to big discrepancies between budget and accounting data (Høgheim et al. 1989). By concentrating on budgets rather than accounts, an organization enjoys greater freedom in presenting its chosen image, not only internally but also to the outside world, so that even its environment may begin to confuse facts with fiction.

The budget decision usually comes as the final stage in a long budget process. In very open organizations such as public agencies at the national or municipal level, the whole budgetary process as well as the final decision usually receives a good deal of attention in the media; this is often the most important forum in which organizations can talk about themselves to an audience that can really hear them, and that hears them clearly. It is also easy to conduct politics in the budget context, that is to produce inconsistent talk. By definition a budget is concerned with the future, and it is not embarrassed by realities which may be difficult for people to disagree about. It is also easy to disagree in connection with the budget, since it is concerned with a continuous variable, namely money, about which there are as many views as there are coins.

In many public agencies budgeting really does lie at the heart of the policy process. A great deal of interest is devoted to the budget by the organizations themselves as well as by the media. Much of the debate both inside and outside these agencies occurs within the framework of the budget process, and much of the work of the administrators and the decision-makers is concerned with it. Work on the annual budget often continues for most of the year. The link between budget and operations is often weak; neither actual performance nor actual outlay necessarily stick very closely to the budget. But in the organization and the media any interest in actual outcomes as reported in annual reports is often extremely slight. Quite often the administration is unable to use all the money allocated to it. For instance, during the great expansion of the public sector in Sweden during the 1960s and 1970s, this was often the case simply because it was physically impossible to build as quickly, or to employ as many people, as the budget required. The budget provided a platform for promises, and on that platform there was no reason to limit staff numbers or restrict the scope of the promises. In fact the best sort of promises were those which would be impossible to fulfil, since they involved no real consumption of funds.

Thus the chief importance of the budget often seems to have been symbolical. Work on the budget provided an important platform for the reflection of inconsistencies in talk and decisions, while actions remained pretty loosely linked to the budgetary decisions. But the usefulness of the budget process to politics and its symbolical value both depended on the availability of more money than would be possible to spend. In more recent years, however, this has not been a typical state of affairs in the public organizations of western Europe. On the contrary, the low level of general economic growth has also limited the growth of tax revenues, turning money into an increasingly scarce resource. In this situation the kind of behaviour described above tends to create financial difficulties. For national governments whose institutional arrangements permit them to spend more money than they have coming in, the result has almost without exception been a budget deficit. In other public agencies without the ability to generate long-term deficits, and where the shortage of money has thus been more tangible, the results have been different.

The lack of money has made it harder to satisfy a variety of demands by taking concrete action. It has thus become more important to produce inconsistent talk and decisions; the debate has become increasingly lively. But it also became more difficult to exploit the budget as an arena for politics, since it was necessary to limit the number of decisions which might call for big outlays. On the contrary, there was every reason for accepting a common interpretation of the role of the budget, namely that it can be used as a way of controlling action and containing expenditure. This would also imply a closer link between budget and action. Below I discuss the role of the budget in a case of municipal budgeting under perceived conditions of scarcity.

BUDGETING UNDER STAGNATION

Ulston is a small municipality in Sweden. The authority employs a workforce of roughly 5,000 and at the beginning of the 1980s was reporting a turnover of around £65 million. Local taxes were high and the municipality had a heavy public debt. Like all Swedish municipalities Ulston set its own local tax rates in the form of a proportional rate on incomes, which in 1980 in Ulston was a little over 17 per cent; if the county council tax is included, the rate was over 31 per cent, and this meant that Ulston had one of the highest tax rates in the country. The residents also had plenty of experience of tax increases, most recently in 1980. A great many services were still inadequate: child care had fallen badly behind, many buildings and whole districts in the centre of the town needed renovating or rebuilding, the administration was scattered among innumerable different locations often in dilapidated buildings, and the care of the elderly was expected to make heavy demands in the future.

The political situation in the municipality had long been unstable. At election time only a few hundred votes separated the non-Socialist and Socialist blocs. The ruling majority in the council was always changing; after a period of Socialist government, the non-Socialist bloc won the election in 1979.

During the election the non-Socialist parties had promised to cancel the tax increases planned by the Socialists. Their intention was to hold the tax rate at the (high) level it had reached under the previous régime—although the current five-year plan already adopted indicated the necessity of an increase with 1.25 percentage point.

The first budget to be prepared entirely by the new ruling coalition was the budget for 1981. At least three reasons have already been mentioned why it should have been done without raising taxes. First, the tax rate was already the highest in the country. Second, most politicians in the ruling coalition wanted to avoid tax increases, and finally, they had committed themselves to such a policy during the election campaign (a promise which had brought them victory; the Socialists had said they would introduce an increase).

Leading politicians and administrators were all firmly convinced that it should be possible to control the economy and municipal operations by means of the budget. If every effort were made in preparing the budget, they thought, it should be possible to keep taxes at their present level, and to produce a budget that really did control developments, that is one that restricted disbursements during the year so that tax revenues at the present rate would provide sufficient funds.

There seemed to be good reason for this conviction. The tax rate is traditionally established in the budget, and like other decisions the budget is often presented in the normative literature as an effective means of controlling developments in practice. In the normative world the budget has a number of qualities which make it seem like a good instrument of control, particularly if its task is to curtail expenditure. To begin with, the budget is a plan. It is intended to limit the administration's economic freedom of action, so that spending on day-to-day operations is restrained by a lack of money. Second, the plan is also supposed to exert control over the purposes on which the money is spent. At the same time the budget is intended to affect what happens in other arenas: it provides the economic limits to what people can plan and do.

Finally, the budget to some extent abolishes the chronological or sequential aspect of organizational operations; it imposes a sort of simultaneity; actions which will be realized at different times are balanced against one another at a single moment. When resources are scarce, this means that certain activities will appear to be mutually exclusive. If we do A we cannot do B. There is thus a strong incentive to exclude some activities.

This highlights the minus side of the budget operation: it is not only an enabling instrument, making it possible to produce something; it also imposes the sacrifice of something else. The expenditure-orientation of the budget has much the same effect; expenses rather than results are described and measured.

The leading politicians in Ulston soon realized that budgets in the real world can look very different from this, and can have other effects. They sent directives to all departments demanding a cut in costs. The budget negotiations then began, lasting as usual for almost a year. But the result of the process was very different from the intentions of the leading politicians. The budget finally presented implied heavy cost increases that made it necessary to raise taxes again. The budget included a 0.5 percentage point tax increase, bringing the total rate up to around 32 per cent. At the same time public borrowing rose again. Nonetheless the budget indicated a predicted loss of liquidity amounting to about £1.5 million.

The new ruling coalition had failed. The budget process in Ulston did not put a stop to further expansion or to tax increases. Nor did it lead to any cost reductions. And what was more, the result was a budget that proved to be too capacious: when the budget year was over the financial accounts showed a budget surplus of more than £1 million, which was a record, as well as being the equivalent of a tax *reduction* of over 1 percentage point. Thus, although it turned out that taxes could have been cut, they had nonetheless been increased. In the next two subsections I will explain how this result could come about.

ROLES AND ACTORS IN THE BUDGET PROCESS

The budget process in Ulston was not particularly unusual. Its most uncommon aspect was perhaps the general conditions of the organization, which was wealthy (empowered to raise taxes from fairly rich taxpayers) but operating in a situation of uncertainty (as shown below). In other words it illustrates Wildavsky's missing (1975) category, the combination of richness and uncertainty—and it was not surprising that such a position resulted in a surplus. But the interest of using Ulston as an empirical illustration is that the budget process was in fact a fairly standard one. It included roles similar to those indicated in budget theory, and the people occupying these roles faced situations that are common to many organizations. We can now examine some of these common characteristics to provide the background necessary to our discussion of the role of responsibility allocation in decision-making.

Roles: Guardians, Champions, and Hoarders

Budgeting theory (Wildavsky 1974) describes the budget as a process of bargaining between actors pursuing different interests and occupying different roles. This was indubitably the case in Ulston, where we found advocates or champions of the various operations as well as guardians of the cash box.

We cannot expect actors playing the role of champions to bother themselves about the balance sheet total, or about whether their precious projects might mean an increase in taxes. That is the guardians' job. Thus, if Ulston was to keep its present tax rate, the guardians would have had to be strong and there should preferably have been many of them. However, as in most organizations, the guardians in Ulston were few in number. The role of the guardian is traditionally played mainly by the top management, while the various departments assume the champion role.

In Ulston the politicians on the executive committee who belonged to the non-Socialist majority assumed the guardian role. The members of the opposition, on the other hand, were committed champions. An opposition does not have the same necessity to urge thrift, since their budget proposals are not expected to be implemented. In this case the opposition also thought taxes should be increased, so they saw plenty of scope for both current and future operations. They had even more scope than could be exploited, according to the most optimistic plans of the various departments. In this way the executive committee in its guardian role was substantially weakened when it came to battling with the champions in the various branches of the administration.

The situation was not improved by the role that the members of the various special committees chose to play. The politicians on these committees can be envisaged, at least in principle, as playing either the guardian or the champion role. They can either see themselves as representing the executive committee and the council, checking that the administrators keep within the prescribed limits and so on, or they can see themselves as representatives of the schools, the roads or whatever it may be, seeing it as their task to provide for the relevant interests in the best possible way.

In Ulston almost all the politicians on the various committees chose to be champions. They sought to ensure that their own departments received a larger portion—or at least not a smaller one—of the available resources. Their choice of role naturally made saving even more difficult, since it meant that the champions appeared not only in the opposition parties but also in the ruling coalition. It was not uncommon to hear people referring to the 'schools party', the 'roads party', etc. that is the clash of interests between the members of different committees was often stronger than the conflict between the regular political parties.

There was always a majority in favour of growth: champions always far outnumbered guardians, both as a whole and in the respective parties. Nor were the champions trying to promote their own demands against the demands of other departments. On the contrary, in this context there was a marked sense of loyalty and consideration for one another. Even in interviews no one was prepared to say which departments they thought had received too much money. So it was left entirely to the guardians to strike the balance between the different departments, and they were unable to exploit the knowledge and arguments that the various committee members certainly possessed about one another's operations. Such loyalty could of course hamper the arguments of any individual department in favour of expanding its own operations, but disloyalty might jeopardize the expansion of the whole administration.

For many reasons it is natural for committee members to assume the champion role. For instance, people are generally recruited on to committees because they already have an interest in, say, schools or roads, and they could easily get arguments for their cause from the relevant department. It must have been particularly easy to assume the role of champion in a period of stagnation: if an operation seems likely to face a cutback, it is all the more important to defend it. Another reason for adopting the champion role in this case was the flexibility of the cash limits set by the the council for the various committees. However much the guardians declared the limits could not be changed, everyone thought of preparing the budget process as a chance not only for adjusting costs to cash limits, but also for influencing the limits themselves. It thus seemed natural to committee members to try to increase the limits set for their own particular sphere of interest, which then made it impossible for them to act as guardians vis-à-vis the administration.

But champions and guardians were not the only roles that were played. Naturally the officials in the finance office did not play the champion role. Nor, however, did they really act as guardians. They were certainly trying to get the departments to save and to restrict their demands, that is they aimed to hold back costs. But they worked just as hard to get revenues increased, mainly by increasing taxes. The aim was a budget surplus. Their goal thus resembles the one generally assigned by economists to entrepreneurs: namely to maximize profit. They were playing the role of the hoarder. They wanted to produce a capacious budget; a budget that should if possible yield a surplus, and certainly one that would avoid a deficit. A capacious budget leaves room for manoeuvres now, and provides resources for an uncertain future.

In Ulston there were naturally good reasons for adopting a hoarder role, not least the large debts which had been accumulated and which now represented a heavy burden. The finance office was in a strong position, particularly when it came to discussing revenue requirements. These were the officers who analysed changes in the economic situation of the municipality and forecast how they would affect costs and revenues. The hoarders employed two main instruments: one for restraining costs and one for increasing revenues. On the cost-containing front this meant recommending concrete expedients for saving. On the revenue side they talked a lot about tax levels, seeking to establish certain expectations of future tax increases in people's minds. They did this in the five-year plan, which they had produced and which had been accepted by the council; it showed an awkward 'imbalance' in the future. And they also did it in their budget guidelines for the next year, which threw cold water on any hope of keeping taxes at the present rate.

The hoarders were successful when it came to protecting revenues, but this immediately complicated their other goal, namely to hold back costs: the expectation that taxes were anyway going to be increased provided the champions with arguments and filled them with optimism.

Actors—Their Values, Knowledge, Expectations, and Organization

The politicians' view of their role is important to an understanding of the budget process described here. Almost all the politicians drew a line between 'politics' and 'saving'. By politics they meant inventing and deciding new activities. Given this definition, there was deplorably little scope for politics when saving was the order of the day. Saving was perceived as a really tough option. Some decisions to save were almost impossible to make. 'I don't want to be remembered as the one who stopped the new museum,' as one leading politician put it.

Some people knew much more than others about municipal operations and the possibility of effecting savings. Naturally the heads of departments knew a great deal more about such things than the central politicians and officials. It was far more difficult for the central units to see where cuts could or should be made, than it had been previously for them to see where increases could or should be allowed. The departments could always help them in their search for growth areas. The guardians suspected that there must be ways of improving efficiency in the departments, but they were not knowledgeable enough themselves to hit on any appropriate measures. Committee members had a little more knowledge, but this did not help the guardians, as these politicians had assumed the champion role.

The different levels of knowledge as between guardians and champions is a typical aspect of budget processes. The guardians are all too likely to have just the amount of knowledge that makes savings difficult: if you know nothing about an operation, you can easily convince yourself that there must be plenty of scope for saving, and if you know a lot about it you have a good chance of seeing concrete opportunities for saving; but if you just know a little bit, it is more difficult to see how savings can be made.

Budgeting is a planning process in which expectations of the future are of central importance. They include expectations about the results of the budget process itself and about economic conditions during the budget year. In Ulston all the leading actors had firmly expected a tax increase to be necessary, despite the non-Socialist majority's express ambition to avoid this. As we have already seen, this expectation was confirmed by the finance office, not least in their five-year plan. The effects of this plan on expectations were very considerable. In the five-year plan the necessity for a 0.75 percentage point increase in the taxes for 1981 had been put on record. When the tax rate was contained at 0.5 percentage point many people perceived this as a 0.25 percentage point reduction! To them the plan was more real than the facts of life. Moreover this provided an excellent argument for the majority coalition to counter any charges that they had failed to keep their election promise.

Expectations engendered by the plan became so firmly rooted that people seem to have found it difficult or uninteresting to distinguish plans from reality. It took three interviews with various financial officers before I discovered that what some people were referring to as estimated cost savings were actually reductions compared with the (expansive) plan, but not compared with present costs! In order to discover whether there was any real reduction, further complicated calculations were required. Very few of the others interviewed were able to say how the 'cost savings' had been calculated.

Despite the powerful impact of the long-term plan on expectations, and consequently on the results of the budget process, the politicians showed comparatively little interest in the revision of the plan, which they were supposed to undertake each year. They concentrated instead on the immediate year's budget. After all, they thought, a decision in the long-term plan was not 'binding'.

The hoarders also benefited from the great uncertainty that prevailed. People were uncertain about various factors which were outside the municipality's control. Above all there was great uncertainty about what measures the national government would impose to enforce saving. Several government proposals were put forward during the budget process, and more were expected. It was difficult to predict exactly what measures would be imposed, and what their impact on the municipal economy might be. As a result of this uncertainty many people felt it would be safest to allow for margins in the budget; and at any rate the uncertainty provided the hoarders with good arguments. Even at the municipal departmental level the uncertainty could be used as an argument for seeking more money; the real estate department, for instance, could plead caution in cutting back their allotment, in view of the unpredictability of future oil prices.

THE ALLOCATION OF RESPONSIBILITY

The guardians' main instrument for controlling the budget was their right—and their duty—to make budget decisions. One major reason why it was difficult for them to acquire any real influence by exploiting this tool was the significant role of responsibility in the budget process: like other decisions, the budget is a question not only of distributing money but also of allocating responsibility.

During times of growth it is often quite easy to assume responsibility for various municipal activities, particularly in the budget process which is geared to future plans; dissatisfaction and criticism do not generally arise until some activity is actually being carried out. The sort of questions that are usually discussed, particularly in expansive budgets, are concerned with marginal increases in resources, that is new undertakings, or perhaps improvements in some currently criticized operation. In periods of stagnation, on the other hand, responsibility can easily become a heavy and unwanted burden. It can hardly ever be pleasant to bear the responsibility for cutting allowances, terminating activities, or making substantial cutbacks in budget applications.

There are two ways of avoiding this pain. One is not to take any cost-cutting action; the other is to avoid any responsibility for it. The disadvantage of the first method is that the overall budget is likely to be too generous; to the guardians the second method must therefore be preferable. For the champions, however, it is much better to let the guardians bear the responsibility for the cutbacks, thus reducing the risk that they will ever take place. The guardians would not have the courage to assume responsibility for them. The struggle between guardians and champions thus becomes essentially a question of the distribution of responsibility.

Responsibility is something assigned to us by other people, and it is connected with the blame or credit for some particular action or happening that is supposed to accrue to us. We are responsible for an action if we are regarded as having caused it to happen, for instance if we made the decision that it should take place. The extent of our responsibility depends ultimately on two factors: the importance ascribed to our own part in the particular context, and the conspicuousness of the relation between ourselves and the action concerned. If we want to play down our responsibility, we can point out that we share it with several others. Alternatively we can point out that we did not cause the action, for instance because we did not make any decision about it.

Since responsibility is something we possess in the eyes of other people, the responsibility for a particular action can only be ascribed to us in so far as the action is seen to have taken place. So a third way of avoiding responsibility is to try to make the action less obvious or visible.

The guardians in Ulston employed two main strategies, one involving the rejection of responsibility and one involving its assumption. The first was to call for savings and to threaten cuts in grants without involving themselves in the specifics of the administration's handling of the situation. Thus they attacked the administration on the grants side, hoping to avoid responsibility for the individual cutbacks. They were then accused by the departmental heads of having an unprofessional approach, for not caring whether things worked out or not. Committee members provided a suitable channel for the transmission of such messages since they knew just about enough, and yet did not know too much, to see that the cutbacks were unworkable.

Because of the difficulties involved in the first strategy the guardians turned to the second, which meant attacking the administration on the operational side. The idea was to compensate for the assumption of considerable responsibility by acquiring more knowledge. The guardians would make the decisions about cutbacks and thus assume responsibility for them, but they would also try to find the cuts for which it would be least painful to bear the responsibility or, better still, to look for ways of improving efficiency, since having responsibility for efficiency was no bad thing. They scrutinized every item of the budget in their discussions with the individual departments during the final budget negotiations. Some cost-cutting was achieved by discontinuing certain operations or investment projects. This approach left even less scope for improving efficiency than the first method. And it was also difficult to include any really radical cutbacks. Once again 'practice took over from politics', as one politician put it. 'Practice' meant looking at operations through the eyes of the administrators, and recognizing just how difficult or impossible it was to save. Consequently, some of the departments adopted a policy of willingly giving the guardians information about details, as a way of avoiding cutbacks.

Proposals and Arguments as Strategies

The chief response of the champions to the cash limits proposed by the guardians was not only to invoke the difficulty or impossibility of saving, but also to counter with some special proposals of their own. They declared that if savings must be made they should be substantial and concentrated to a single area. It was better to discontinue one operation altogether than to reduce standards across the board. Such discontinuations—the closing of a leisure centre for example—are highly visible to the world at large, and the formal decisions are taken by the politicians in the executive committee and the council. So the central politicians, that is the guardians, bear a heavy burden of responsibility.

The guardians' proposals were different. They preferred the idea of saving by making minor cuts over the whole range of operations. Their favoured proposal was what they called 'the little axe', that is that all departments should save roughly the same amount, for example 3 per cent per year, but without saying how it should be done. Such a slight lowering of standards would be perceived as the responsibility of the departments; if holes in the road are not repaired people do not ring the top politicians to complain, they call the highways department. Moreover the guardians suspected that efficiency could probably be improved in most areas, and this would make any lowering of standards, and certainly any closures, unnecessary.

Thus the champions threatened the guardians, declaring that if they did not get enough money, closures would be necessary, and the closures or cancellations they suggested were often extremely visible and sure to be unpopular; in previous years the education department had suggested stopping school milk. Now it was being suggested that the recreation committee should cancel the grants to certain associations. Such grants were made direct from the finance office after a council decision. There was no risk of the administration or the committees being ascribed the responsibility for such a measure.

The champions' threats were largely effective. The only major closure decision concerned an unprofitable minor service facility. But even this met with violent protests from the opposition, which made a big political issue of the shutdown. In other words it was made very clear where the responsibility lay.

Responsibility is concerned not only with *what* people believe others are doing, but also *why* they think they are doing it. For example more responsibility is ascribed to someone who is assumed to have carried out (or decided on) an action of his 'own free will', than to someone who has been 'compelled' to do it. It is important to note that the actor's own motives for his action are uninteresting in this context; it is the motives which others ascribe to him which matter. These ascribed motives can be affected by argument, that is presenting explanations of actions and decisions which can be used in the process of allocating responsibility. An actor can use such explanations to soften the link between himself and his action, or to present the action in a positive light so that it becomes a good thing to be held responsible for it. In Ulston the actors tried to steer the distribution of responsibility not only by proposing what actions were to be taken but also by arguing their case.

For instance the actors would deliberate on the savings theme: was it a good thing or a bad thing to save, and why did they want to save? On the first of these points the champions would talk about the importance of various municipal activities, not only to demonstrate the negative aspect of cutbacks and retrenchments but also in terms of the much needed jobs that these same activities provided. The guardians meanwhile talked about the negative aspects of a tax increase. And on the second point they referred to the poor economy of the country as a whole as well as in the municipality, and generally tried to spread a sense of 'crisis'. It was not their fault that costs would have to be cut. As a result of the proposed across-the-board cuts, they were simply transferring the savings inflicted by environmental conditions to the departments, without really making any decisions themselves. But when the opposition (and even the hoarders) pointed out that it would be possible to increase taxes, then it became difficult for the guardians to claim that they 'had' to make cuts: if they had decided *not* to increase taxes, they would also have been held largely responsible for the cutbacks which would then have become necessary.

To cut down in a general way in order to prevent tax increases seemed at least to some actors to be a positive thing, that is they did not mind being held responsible for it. But to cut back, or refuse to increase an allocation in some specific case, was not pleasant. Thus the guardians found it very difficult to counter the arguments of the individual departments. Their own argument about the country's generally poor economy was not much help. The champions simply claimed that even if the economy as a whole was in a poor way there was still no need to save in their particular field. It was not impossible to increase taxes or charges or the borrowing debt (particularly by the little bit necessary in order to avoid one particular cutback). And in any case it was always possible to make a cut somewhere else. And when the guardians claimed that the same saving was being made everywhere else, they were still talking about a decision of their own. In other words, if a cut was made in a particular sphere of operations, it was the guardians who had freely chosen to make it and they must bear the responsibility.

The champions also argued that they were not responsible for the fact that no cuts would be made in their department. They referred to a series of conditions out of their control, such as laws forcing them to produce certain services or general price increases making their operations more expensive. The champions also argued that there were close links between money and service—less money would always result in proportionately less service. In other words, they excluded the possibility of increased efficiency, thereby emphasizing the only negative element in the proposed cutbacks.

Generally speaking the champions had the best arguments, in that it was easier for them to demonstrate that the negatively charged responsibility belonged to the other party, namely the guardians. The guardians did not have much to set against these arguments. It is difficult to prove that an operation is not necessary, or that outside circumstances make some specific cutback unavoidable, and it is very hard to show that the champions are responsible—particularly if the guardians make the formal decisions on individual cuts.

As it turned out, the guardians later found it quite easy to justify why they finally decided to increase taxes. They pointed out that they were still keeping within the limits recommended by the national government. They felt they had done a good job at saving, for a first attempt; it is difficult to change everything in one year, nor is it possible to make an abrupt break with everything the administration has planned. In other words the result was not so bad, and in any case they were not fully responsible for it.

'Division of Labour' for Expansion

In many ways the budget process in Ulston was determined by two factors: the ease with which the guardians could be held responsible, and the champions' superior knowledge. All ways of saving (closures or cancellations, lowering of standards or improvements in efficiency) were blocked by a kind of division of labour between guardians, champions, and hoarders.

Guardians can most easily be held responsible for closures or cancellations. These are the most visible of all savings, and those which are most obviously the result of central political decisions. The guardians in Ulston were often unable to cope with the heavy responsibility that such measures involve, and therefore tried as far as possible to prevent them from occurring. This left the lowering of standards, or improvements in efficiency. But the champions were very good at pointing out the impossibility of any acceptable reduction in standards or improvements in efficiency, safe in the knowledge that the guardians did not know enough about the complicated issues. Thus the champions ensured that there would be no lowering of standards and no improvements in efficiency. Whereas the guardians' role was to prevent closures or cancellations, and the champions' to prevent a lowering of standards or improvements in efficiency, the role of the hoarders seems to have been to promote this 'division of labour' by encouraging expansion. If ample resources are made available, the necessity for any cutbacks immediately becomes less urgent. The hoarders found it almost as difficult as the guardians to push through cutbacks, but it was quite easy for them to see that more resources were made available. This was because they held the purse strings, they handled the financial reporting, and they made the budget estimates—in short, they were the experts on the municipal economy, and when they claimed that money was lacking and a financial crisis was pending no one had the knowledge to argue against them. The hoarders also had a lot of good arguments showing the advantages of capacious budgeting. 'In these uncertain and difficult times, it is important that the municipal economy should be strong and resistant.'

The result of the budget process was that expansion and tax increases both continued, which meant that at the end of the budget year there was a large cash surplus. The threat of a 'poor' economy had resulted in a surplus. The champions had succeeded in getting so much money that they had been unable to spend it all. Both champions and hoarders had done well.

The budget process in Ulston illustrates clearly how difficult it can be for decision-makers to exert influence just because they must make the formal decisions. The guardians certainly had little influence on the design of the budget; and the major impediment to their influence was the very fact of their right and duty to make decisions! The responsibility generated by their decision-making impeded any influence they might otherwise have had.

CONTROL—SUPPLY AND DEMAND

The budget process in Ulston shows how the responsibility attaching to decisions can have paradoxical effects on control in organizations. When the guardians became aware of economic problems, they were no longer interested in the kind of decoupling of decisions and actions which had been typical of the expansion period, and which involved them in decisions rather than action. Now, instead, they wanted to use the budget to limit the amount of action and consequently also the cost, in other words to link decision and action together.

Paradoxically, however, this ambition on the part of the guardians resulted in bargaining strategies aimed at loosening the link between decisions and actions. The guardians were trying to avoid deciding exactly what actions should be carried out. They preferred to indicate general economic cash limits to the departments, without saying how these should be achieved. They tried to get the champions to make the decisions about what specific actions the money should be used for. In order to tackle the economy as a whole, they tried to abstain from controlling individual actions. The supply of control was clearly limited.

But the demand for control was all the more marked. The champions tried to get the guardians to say exactly what cutbacks they were to make, hoping that if the guardians were forced into a control situation they would not be able to achieve much in the way of cutbacks (perhaps none at all). This proved to be an accurate assessment of the situation; the guardians turned out to be almost wholly incapable of controlling cutbacks; all they could control was expansion.

Thus there was a shortage of control: the demand was greater than the supply. It was the very people who would be controlled who were demanding control, while those who would exert the control were trying to avoid it. We appear to have a situation here that contradicts most theories of control and power: it is generally assumed that there is an ample supply of control but little demand for it, that there will always be at least some people who want to exert control and who strive to acquire it, while those who are exposed to their strivings for control will try to evade it. The seeming paradox in this case can be explained by the fact that guardians and champions were both fully aware that control over specific actions would mean less control over the economy as a whole—either the municipal economy in the case of the guardians or the department economy in the case of the champions.

The champions won the battle to force others to assume control, and the guardians finally decided on a number of expansive measures. Thus decision and action were mutually consistent; decisions were coupled to actions, but, not in such a way as to put the decision-makers in control of the actions. Rather, those who were directly involved in the actions steered the decision-makers towards the decisions they wanted. As a result of these decisions, the actions acquired the financial and other kinds of support needed for their implementation from the central politicians and administrators.

The explanation of all these effects is that decisions generate responsibility. In periods of expansion the budget decision granted responsibility but little influence; the departments were allowed considerable freedom, and there was often little consistency between specific decisions in the budget and in the actions actually performed. Even when budget and action agreed, the process normally inclined to yield more responsibility than influence: the budget decision may refer to the whole operation, but in designing the budget the discussions generally revolve around minor changes in grants compared with the previous year (so-called incrementalism). During the period of stagnation the relation between responsibility and influence became more crucial to the guardians: they wanted to avoid responsibility for cutbacks while also wanting to influence the content of the budget so that reasonably appropriate cutbacks would in fact be achieved. But responsibility inevitably attached to them, because it was after all their duty to make budget decisions, and this impeded their influence. Because of the negative effects of bearing responsibility for cutbacks, the guardians no longer either wanted or dared to make any decisions on the subject.

It is difficult to use decisions as a way of acquiring influence, but it is also easy to acquire responsibility in this way. Now we have also found that responsibility can directly influence the content of a decision, that is the choice which the organization makes. By putting most of the responsibility on the decision-makers, the champions were able to influence not only the decision-makers' choices but also what the guardians said they wanted to achieve. Even preferences appear to have been affected by the burden of responsibility. Thus, once again, it was not simply an implementation problem, caused by actors refusing to obey the decisions of the decision-makers.

What is more, the decisions of the guardians about continuing or expanding operations were not binding on the champions. If they wanted to make some cutback of their own during the budget year, they were free to do so. The guardians would be only too grateful, even if the champions had declared those very cutbacks to be impossible during the budget process. Moreover, as in the expansive period, the budget process generated a surplus of money both centrally and in the departments—money which was used or which could have been used for further operations.

Presumably the influence of the guardians would have been greater if they had not been lured into trying to control the content of the budget by their decisions. If they had actually succeeded in restricting their decisions to indicating cash limits for the different departments, and had not included the content of the operations in their decisions, they would have had a better chance of achieving at least one of their goals: to limit expenditure and thus also the tax rate. More influence can be acquired by avoiding the decision-maker role than by shouldering it; responsibility can impede influence.

Thus the budget process was concerned with control, even if the control did not proceed in the same direction as is suggested in normative budget literature. The top was controlled by the bottom. The budget became a question of financing—not a process in which the central level allocated money to the local level according to its preferences, but a process whereby the local level ensured that its operations would be financed.

One of the main reasons why responsibility was so important in the budget was that the relevant talk and decisions were being played before external as well as internal audiences. They not only affected internal affairs; they also constituted organizational outputs to be observed by the world outside. The decision-makers were not only responsible in the eyes of the organization's own members but also in the eyes of the public which was to enjoy the services and pay the taxes. Budget processes are also concerned with an organization's relations with its environment. This aspect of the process will be discussed in the next subsection.

BUDGETING AS AN INSTRUMENT FOR FINANCING

As was noted in the introduction to this chapter, budget processes provide suitable instruments for the production of hypocrisy. In one sense the Ulston budget process produced less hypocrisy than organizations in periods of expansion are capable of. The link between budget decisions and subsequent actions in Ulston became much firmer than it had been, in that a greater number of the budget decisions were actually carried out. As we have seen, this was because both guardians and champions perceived resources as scarce; consequently the guardians tried to limit the number of decisions about expenditure, and the champions tried to ensure that financing really was available for the actions they wanted to realize.

But in another sense the process produced more hypocrisy. The external demands on the organization, as perceived by its members, were inconsistent: the organization was under pressure to reduce taxes, or at least to hold them at the current level, while it was also being asked to provide more and better services. The budget processes reflected both these demands. A lot of talk about cost reductions was produced but in practice services actually continued to expand. This was typical behaviour in Sweden at the time: there was a great deal of talk about efficiency and savings on all kinds of occasions devoted to this topic, but virtually no improvements in efficiency were ever actually made (Rombach 1986) and expansion continued.

Høgheim et al. (1989) reported similar results in Norwegian municipalities. One major difference, however, was that budgets were being used there as proof of saving. The decisions in the budget implied continual reductions in total operations, while actual developments as reported in the accounting records revealed uninterrupted growth. This hypocrisy was produced by fixing attention on the future, so that both the actors themselves and external observers in the media and the state organizations stuck to the budget figures in comparing different years.

External Financing

The budget process is thus well suited to the job of maintaining legitimacy in inconsistent environments; but it can also have other more direct effects: it can operate as a financing instrument not only internally but even externally as well.

The model of the budget process which I have described here can be used not only for describing the struggle between organizational levels but also for describing the organization's relations with its environment. In terms of this model the relations between public organizations and taxpayers can be conceived as relations between different roles in the budget process. The organizations can be seen as champions and hoarders, as against the general public acting as guardians. Like the organization's own guardians, the public cannot easily acquire information about the various operations or learn fully to understand them, and this makes it difficult for the public to say no. In their champion role organizations employ a number of classical tricks: they claim that 'activity' is identical to 'money' (if health care is not granted more money, there will simply be less health care); they threaten to discontinue whole operations; they conceal opportunities for improving efficiency; they describe in lurid detail the effects of any reduction of their grants, and they are careful to ensure that they have no competitors, who might be able to show that the same operation could be run more cheaply. As hoarders, the organizations obscure their resources in incomprehensible accounting systems and explain that there is no money, or at least that there will be no money soon when the crisis they have all been talking about actually appears (normally in two years' time).

Financing calls for different strategies, depending on whether it is based on taxes or borrowing, for example. When a company or any other organization wants to borrow money from a bank or to acquire capital by issuing shares, it first has to show that it is solvent. In its share prospectus the company and its future prospects are described in glowing terms. In order to protect creditors or shareholders, various laws and accounting norms are designed to prevent companies and others from exaggerating their economic status. In tax-based financing the reverse strategy obtains: in order to emphasize the need for money it is necessary to describe the organization's economic status in gloomy terms, to claim a present or future shortage of money, to point to a threatening crisis. Nor are there generally the same strict legal rules obstructing organizations from understating their economic status.

The internal struggle for money between guardians, champions, and hoarders makes a strong impact outside the organization, as the whole budget process gets a lot of attention in the media. A typical budget process opens with the guardians telling the champions about the great shortage of money, and the hoarders talking about a threatening financial crisis. The champions are told they must lower their sights. The attentive taxpayer is thus clearly given to understand that the money he has previously paid is now finished and more is needed. A few months later the champions respond, showing just how impossible it would be to save as much as the guardians want without very seriously or even fatally affecting operations. Newspaper headlines shout about all the programmes, so dear to the people, that are going to be abolished. Staff and public are moved to protest, lists of names are collected, demonstrations held. The public recognizes that the only chance of rescuing the particular programme they want most is to give more money to the organization. Some months later it becomes increasingly obvious that taxes or charges must be increased, or at most that they cannot be cut. By the time the final budget decision is reached, most people probably accept it as perfectly sensible and right.

Thus the budget process does not only help the champions to win acceptance from the guardians for the expenditure they crave, but it also helps the organization as a whole to win the understanding of those who will ultimately pay the additional costs. Again the budget process is more successful as an instrument of control from 'the bottom-up' than from 'the top-down', as a financing instrument rather than a means of control by the leaders, since it can alter the way the external contributors perceive the supply of money and the need for it. Thus, once again the budget process can be described not only as a process which shows in a very general way how the organization responds to a variety of demands; it is also a process directly linked to financing.

In Ulston the financing process was very successful: the organization was able to procure much more money than it could spend, a result that Ulston shared with many municipalities in a similar situation. At the same time the budget process was useful in concealing or legitimizing this excess of liquidity since it focused attention on the future, not the present. And in the future today's figures are irrelevant, and money is always in short supply.

Internal Decisions and External Effects

Decision processes offer a natural way of coupling politics to action in organizations. But our discussion has also shown that decisions tend to endow the decision-makers with responsibility rather than influence. We have also seen how responsibility can promote both implementation and financing; in both cases, the decisions help to convince the outside world of the rightness of the organization's actions. Thus, the decisions help to create consistent views in the environment's demands, and it is easier to achieve action once these inconsistencies have been reduced.

The decision processes described here have thus been largely determined by intentions and deliberations concerned with internal conditions; but they have also had external consequences. In the next chapter I describe how decisions in an organization can have a more direct effect on its external relations. And once again the concept of responsibility will be important to our understanding of organizational behaviour.

REFERENCES

Brorström, B. (1982). *Planeringspolitik eller resultatpolitik.* Lund, Sweden: Doxa.

—— (1985). 'Uppföljning och framförhållning—om bokslut och ekonomisk planering i storstadskommuner', in Sven Wiberg, *Ledarskapets förnyelse.* Lund, Sweden: Doxa.

Høgheim, S., Monsen, N., Olsen, R., and Olson, O. (1989). 'The Two Worlds of Management Control', *Financial Accountability and Management*, 5: 163–178.

Olsen, J. P. (1971). 'Local Budgeting: Decision-Making or a Ritual Act', *Scandinavian Journal of Political Studies*, 5: 85–118.

Rombach, B. (1986). *Rationalisering eller prat?* Lund, Sweden: Doxa.

Wildavsky, A. (1974). *The Politics of the Budgetary Process.* Boston, MA: Little Brown.

—— (1975). *Budgeting. A Comparative Theory of Budgetary Processes.* Boston, MA: Little Brown.

6

Industrial Policy as Implementation or Legitimation

Prince Andrew listened attentively to Bagration's colloquies with the commanding officers and the orders he gave them, and to his surprise found that no orders were really given but that Prince Bagration tried to make it appear that everything done by necessity, by accident, or by the will of subordinate commanders, was done, if not by his direct command at least in accord with his intentions. Prince Andrew noticed however that though what happened was due to chance and was independent of the commander's will, owing to the tact Bagration showed, his presence was very valuable. Officers who approached him with disturbed countenances became calm; soldiers and officers greeted him gaily, grew more cheerful in his presence, and were evidently anxious to display their courage before him.

Leo Tolstoy, *War and Peace*, part II, ch. 17.

SOCIETY AS HIERARCHY

In the popular European political debate it is customary to regard the state as a controlling organ. It is assumed that the state controls or at least strives to control large sections of societal development. Society itself is often conceived as a hierarchy, in which the state constitutes the superordinate leadership unit—the same image that is generally used to describe the state's own vast organization, which is also assumed to be hierarchic, that is topped by the politicians who control the work of the ministries, which in turn control the various government offices and boards. Thus, ultimately, the state political system is perceived as controlling society as a whole—a vertical conception which generates a sense of order and meaning. As a result of this hierarchic view, the role of the state in society is discussed in terms borrowed from the world of the individual organization and its leadership. It is assumed that management, that is the political system, is willing and able to change the behaviour of other subordinate actors on a basis of its own 'goals', which bear upon the development of society as a whole. Political decisions are to be 'implemented', thus leading to the fulfilment of the political goals. One of the major problems, however, is that this process is often obstructed, perhaps by an intractable and complicated administration or by opposition and reluctance from other groups of citizens.

Industrial policy is one of many areas in which the hierarchic metaphor recurs. It is assumed that the function of industrial policy is to influence the structure and development of industrial enterprises, to bring them more in line with political preferences regarding employment, expansion, level of technological development, export sales, etc. Such an ambition requires not only that the political system takes the initiative and actively controls the development of individual companies but also that it solves difficult problems—after all, it is rarely at all clear how the desired ends should be attained. Swedish industrial policy has triggered off a wide-ranging normative debate, including sharp criticism of the way the policy is conducted as well as many suggestions about what should be done instead.

According to the hierarchic metaphor industrial policy is something which the political system initiates and carries through. If we abandon this image it becomes more clearly evident that industrial policy calls for the participation of at least two parties, industry and the politicians. Industrial policy can be defined as the interaction between industry and politics. It is not immediately clear which of the two is most interested in industrial policy, which is most active, or which takes the most initiatives. Industry and politicians both conduct industrial policy. Firms often have strong reasons for joining up with the national politicians: the state has money; it is a source of finance which has often proved possible to tap when other sources have run dry. The state has also shown an ability to survive far exceeding that of business companies. In other words the interest of companies in industrial policy is not difficult to understand. The willingness of politicians to join up with corporate enterprise seems more difficult to explain. The hierarchic metaphor—that the role of the politicians is to govern and guide—offers an explanation, but a highly dubious one.

In the following pages I am going to raise some doubts regarding the hierarchic metaphor in the sphere of industrial policy. The hierarchic metaphor presupposes that the state, with the politicians at its head, is *able* and *willing* to control. Both these assumptions will be called in question below.

CAN THE STATE CONTROL INDUSTRY?

The hierarchic metaphor presupposes that the political system of the state can control industry, that the state has qualities and tools which make it able to steer individual companies in the direction it desires. In other words the interaction between state and industry should mean that the state can influence the behaviour of companies in areas which it regards as important.

However, several empirical studies of industrial policy in Sweden have shown that the state's ability to exert control in individual cases is often very small. Neither the type nor the amount of investment undertaken by large Swedish corporations is affected by the substantial state aid which has been received. Rather, this aid tends to finance investments which were anyway going to be made (Gandemo 1983). In making decisions about economic aid to individual companies in trouble during the 1970s, the state was in a weak bargaining position; it was 'practically impossible to say no' (Swedish Government Official Reports 1981: 72).

These results do not seem so surprising when we remember that politicians also have found it very difficult to control their own agencies (Brunsson and Jönsson 1979; Wiberg 1985). A lot of problems arise when the politically composed units seek to influence the activities of the hierarchically ordered administrative units. The political units are built on different principles, and this greatly affects these difficulties in exerting control.

In the same way the state and the business firms represent different forms of organization. The state is a political organization in which the 'management' at least has been composed specifically to reflect and express conflicting norms in its environment and it is important that these conflicts should be openly reported (Brunsson 1986). Companies are more hierarchically organized, with greater emphasis on a homogeneous leadership which strives to promote coordinated action in its organization. Compared with the state, companies are also more closed and more anxious to conceal their internal conflicts from the outside world.

Political and hierarchic organizations have different types of organizational ideology, that is, the views of the members about their organization and its situation are of a different character. Hierarchic organizations tend to have 'strong' organizational ideologies. In hierarchic organizations there are powerful forces striving to inculcate in their members a common, consistent attitude towards crucial issues. The common organizational ideology is often also both precise and complex; the members have fairly exact and detailed knowledge about the area of operations of their organization. Political organizations, on the other hand, tend to have 'weak' organizational ideologies, that is ideologies that are inconsistent, vague, and simple. The definition of a political organization says that its leading members should have at least partly conflicting views about the situation of the organization and about what should be done. The management of a political organization is generally composed primarily on grounds of representativeness rather than of expertise.

A weak ideology is easy to change by disseminating another that is stronger (Brunsson 1985). It is therefore relatively easy for hierarchic organizations to manipulate political ones. Political organizations find it easy to let themselves be influenced; it could even be claimed that this is their central function. They are after all meant to represent the ideas obtaining in their environment.

Individual companies thus have an ideological advantage when they negotiate with the state. This is particularly evident when the bargaining involves large companies and a lot of money. Huge sums are often handled by the political leadership—the government and the parliament; the negotiations are not delegated to the public agencies which are more hierarchically organized and which therefore in principle have a stronger bargaining position. Large companies often possess a kind of monopoly of knowledge; many of the country's experts work within their area of production.

Yet another difficulty dogs the state and the political leadership when it comes to controlling business firms. This is the openness of the state system; virtually all companies and projects can call on the state to handle their problems. The state cannot avoid tackling problems; if it should try to do so, this is seen as the adoption of an active stance vis-à-vis the demands in question. In Sweden the national politicians are regarded as ultimately responsible for almost everything, including the problems of the corporate sector. Unlike most organizations, the state can only answer 'yes' or 'no' to demands it receives from outside—neglecting the demands or to reject them on grounds that they fall outside the organization's responsibilities is simply not a practical possibility. The state has little control over its own agenda.

Because of this openness the political leadership is responsible for positive decisions to support corporate projects—but this is not all. Since even rejections are regarded as active decisions, the politicians are held responsible for these as well. In order to cope with saying 'no', they need arguments which the surrounding world will regard as legitimate. Thus both acceptance and rejection have to be equally well motivated. Strong arguments in favour of approval are willingly supplied by the aid-seekers. But because of the companies' superior knowledge, it is often difficult for the state to find counterarguments which the applicants cannot refute. And without credible counterarguments, the state finds it difficult to justify its refusals.

The story of the BAS investment (Brunsson 1983) illustrates the weakness of the state when it comes to controlling industry. BAS was one of Sweden's largest industrial investments of the 1970s. It commanded a huge amount of state aid, and resulted in total economic failure. The money invested was never recovered; the plant did not even cover its own running costs. The state provided economic aid in two rounds: on the first occasion the politicians responsible in the government were very dubious about whether the project could be profitable, and on the second occasion they were convinced that it was not profitable. On neither occasion, however, did the government see any possibility of refusing to support the project, and this for several reasons.

The government lacked legitimate arguments for a refusal. The BAS project was presented in such a way that it accorded well with the government's own proclaimed strategy, namely to invest in 'futures' industries. According to the very complicated estimates produced by the project management, the project would be profitable. Although the government did not believe this, it could not prove that the estimates were wrong. These had been made by Sweden's leading experts in the relevant product area. No equivalent foreign experts were available, and would in any case have belonged to rival companies.

The government was approached at a late stage, when a great deal of money had already been spent, houses on a suitable piece of land had already been demolished, the project had gathered a good many supporters in the trade unions and the municipality, and expectations in the region were high—the project was expected to come off. Thus a lot of people already felt bound to the project, and were assuming it would be realized. In such a situation it was very difficult for the government to turn it down. And in fact the government realized a rejection on its part would probably be overturned in the parliament where there was much interest in supporting industrial expansion and little in protecting the national budget from major expenditure. In other words the state could not bring itself to say 'no', although politicians and civil servants in the Government Office considered the project to be extremely doubtful or even downright unacceptable.

Approval was made easier because responsibility was dispersed among several organizations as well as being spread over a long period of time. The government's own decision was split between two occasions, and responsibility for each subdecision was thus diluted. Several organizations had previously taken a number of positive subdecisions about the project, and they thus shared the responsibility for approval with the government.

The BAS project illustrates some of the difficulties facing the state when it comes to exerting control over business companies. These difficulties are a problem for the hierarchic metaphor—but are they actually a problem for the state and its leaders? Does the political system really want to control the business companies? This is the question I shall be addressing in the following section.

THE WILL TO CONTROL—IMPLEMENTATION OR LEGITIMATION?

The hierarchic metaphor presupposes not only that the political leadership of the state can control the business companies, but also that it *wants* to. The metaphor is closely associated with a belief that, unlike most other organizations, a political organization such as the state is geared primarily to influencing conditions outside its own boundaries. While industrial companies, for example, are assumed to be interested solely in their own well-being, the state and the municipalities are assumed to be working unselfishly for the welfare of other people. Moreover, the state in particular is credited with a notable inability to leave things alone; it is assumed to want to change a great variety of material conditions in its environment.

This assumption that political organizations are so very extrovert and change-oriented appears dubious to say the least. The idea seems to have been borrowed from the way political organizations talk about their role and their functions, rather than from any empirical studies of their actual situation. In fact it seems more probable that an organization which bases its legitimacy to such a great extent on reflecting the various ideas obtaining in its environment rather than on taking action, would generally have little real interest in changing its environment. And this applies particularly when changing or improving the environment meets with great or insuperable obstacles.

In this section I discuss some conceivable relations between the state and industry. Using a case study I illustrate the way in which these relations can work out in practice. I differentiate between two possible functions for the state's industrial policy—as implementation or legitimation. Viewed in the light of the hierarchic metaphor, the main function lies in implementation. The state is supposed to make decisions about changes in society, and these decisions are also supposed to be carried out. A whole branch of research, implementation research, has developed around this approach concerned among other things to discover why so many powerful decisions made in various political assemblies fail to generate the relevant action or to attain the effects of which the decision-makers spoke. If instead the main function of the state is assumed to be legitimation, the perspective is almost the reverse: action by no means represents the only way of achieving legitimacy and it is not even certain that consistency between decision and action is desirable. Let us now examine the implementation and legitimation perspectives in greater detail.

Different Forms of Implementation and Legitimation

In an implementation perspective it is action and its effects that are the important result of politics. The political system is interested in the first instance in influencing other systems apart from its own. According to this view, the obstacles to action or to the realization of decisions lie outside the political system, in the state's own administrative apparatus or in the industrial system.

The political system has firm intentions for the development of industry, and it strives to solve problems and to exert control.

Even if in practice industrial policy could be understood largely in an implementation perspective, it still does not need to possess all these attributes. Instead we could conceive of different forms of implementation policy, embodying different amounts of 'implementation attributes'. The most extreme form would then be *problem-solving*. Such a policy would mean that the political system tries to solve problems in the industrial system, that is, the state is equipped not only with powerful intentions (which identify the important problems and possible solutions), but also with activities geared to discovering the best possible—or at least some acceptable—actions, which should then be carried out.

In a less extreme variant the political system aims not at problem-solving but at *control*. Even if the political system does not initiate action with a view to solving industrial problems, it may still want to help to determine what action is taken. The political system wants to control what happens, and it is active in taking the initiative.

In the mildest form of implementation policy the political system still expects to see that certain measures are taken, but it does not actively concern itself with controlling what these actions are. By making decisions, or in some other way, the political system *supports* certain actions. The actions need not be controlled by the political system; even less need they represent solutions to problems which the politicians themselves have put forward.

Thus we have three kinds of implementation policy—problem-solving, control, and support. In all these, action is the essential result, but the political system's link with the action varies in its strength. In a legitimation perspective, on the other hand, actions taken or measures adopted are not the major result of the operations of the political system. Action is not an end; at most it is a means. The vital result is now legitimacy.

A legitimation policy involves activities on the part of the political system directed towards creating legitimacy for itself. The main strategy of the political organization for creating its own legitimacy is to reflect in its structure, its processes, and its production the norms and values and interests that obtain in the environment (Brunsson 1986). This represents a *direct* way of creating legitimacy. But legitimacy can also be created indirectly, through the agency of the industrial system. This indirect aspect of legitimacy is connected with the question of the *responsibility* resting with the political system.

Increasingly often the political system is given responsibility for industrial problems. To be responsible for something means being regarded as a cause. If, for instance, the political system is responsible for the unsatisfactory state of industry, it means that the political system is regarded as having caused the situation or of being in a position to correct it (but of having chosen not to do so). This responsibility associates the political system with the industrial system, and means that the legitimacy of the political system becomes dependent on the legitimacy of the industrial system. If industry enjoys a high degree of legitimacy, there is no political problem; but if the industrial system is lumbered with qualities of a strongly negative kind and is thus low on legitimacy, then the political responsibility becomes problematic. In such a situation the political system can acquire legitimacy in two diametrically opposite ways: either by trying to dispose of its responsibility for the situation, or by accepting responsibility but endowing the situation with greater legitimacy.

If the political system disposes of its responsibility, then it detaches itself from the industrial system. We can call the rejection of responsibility the destabilizing line. Applied more extensively it means that the political system distances itself from major aspects of societal development, which can generate conflict and instability in the industrial system and perhaps in the long run in the political system too.

The assumption of responsibility can then be said to represent the stabilizing strategy. On the whole it has been the main strategy of political systems in many industrial countries, since the Second World War, and it has led to what is sometimes called 'overload', that is the political system has shouldered responsibility for almost everything from the state of the world economy and industrial development to the problems of the young and house-building technology.

If the political system adopts the responsibility-assuming strategy, it can increase its legitimacy by steering people's ideas about the industrial situation in a positive direction. This can in fact be done by attempting to influence the industrial system by implementing various measures. The strategy then consists of implementation by way of problem-solving, with all the difficulties that this can give rise to. But people's ideas about a situation can be changed without there being any material alteration in the situation itself. Exerting influence exclusively on people's ideas in this way can be dubbed *situational legitimation*. Situational legitimation means that the political system is legitimized and at the same time its environment is affected, but this is influence of a different kind from the influence resulting from an implementation policy.

Tools

Three types of tool for creating legitimacy can be distinguished: talk, decisions, and action. Talk is an important tool for political organizations. Using this tool people can describe situations as positive or negative, they can describe their own role, they can influence their responsibility or provide arguments for decisions and actions and situations, and much else besides. Decisions are generally seen as a choice between different action alternatives. A person who has made a decision has therefore also made a choice and has thus at least helped to cause an action or an event and to be regarded as a cause of something means being assigned responsibility for it. The decision process can be designed in such a way as to reinforce or weaken the decision-maker's responsibility and legitimacy. Different types of action, for example action initiated by different persons, can also affect legitimacy in different ways.

Talk and decisions are tools which the political system can also use when it comes to implementing action. In order to carry out an action it is often important to be able to describe and justify it in a way that is appropriate to the person who is to perform it. The way in which decisions are made is also important; for instance, the decision process may aim to bind the implementor to the decision, and the decision can express the political system's commitment to the action, and its determination that the action really will be carried out. And in fact the action itself can also be an instrument of implementation: recommendations that are differently designed may be more, or less, likely to be carried out. There may be a difference between suggestions that are vaguely or operationally defined, between proposals involving the payment of money for an operation or those that describe more directly how it should be carried out, between actions to be taken via the administration or directly by industry itself. Money payments to the public agencies with vague directives about what they are to be used for probably belong to those actions most likely to be performed, but they involve the least control and the least specific problem-solving.

To summarize: industrial policy can function either as a way of effecting the implementation of action in the industrial system, or as a means of legitimizing the political system. An implementation policy may concern problem-solving, control, or simply support for action. The legitimation policy may concern direct legitimation, legitimation by influencing responsibility, or situational legitimation. The main tools available to the political system are talk, decisions, and actions.

An Illustration

To illustrate this discussion of implementation and legitimation I briefly describe and analyse a case of state industrial policy—PLACE. The PLACE was presented by one of the Scandinavian governments as their suggestion for saving jobs in a community suffering from severe unemployment. In the

BAS case we could say that the state became a victim of an industrial policy conducted by companies and projects in the industrial system. In the PLACE case the initiative lay to a great extent with the state, and the opportunities for exerting control and steering events could therefore have been expected to be greater.

PLACE—A Description

PLACE is a municipality with high unemployment and extensive state-owned industry; it is also a big recipient of government industrial aid. On several occasions hopes of a more favourable situation for industry and more jobs have been dashed. The government presented a special bill for this community, including various decisions and actions which were to improve the situation there. It was estimated that the measures would cost several hundreds of million pounds. The idea was to restructure a state-owned company in the municipality, which would lead to more unemployment, while at the same time launching an aid package and new investment by the state, which would help to improve the employment situation. How had the government arrived at this comprehensive bill, incorporating decisions about so many measures that would cost so much money?

The story began several years earlier. First the trade unions in the municipality had produced a union programme of action. A little later representatives for the community also raised the question within the government party and persuaded the national party organization to adopt certain declarations about the necessity of tackling unemployment in the area. Representatives of the community then presented the party board with further demands for action. The board decided that a plan of action should be drawn up.

A working group was appointed, including central and local representatives of the party. The central representatives were anxious that any recommendations made should be firmly rooted in the community—what everybody thinks must be important—and the local representatives were anxious that 'the outsiders' should really face up to the problems and the demands that were being raised. Thus a common interest lay behind the way things were organized, whereby the group held discussions with various leading actors in the municipality and the trade unions, thus gathering together virtually all the suggestions that were being made in the community.

It was then a question of deciding which proposals should be included in the plan, and how they should be presented. The plan was to include only promises which would be kept. Where the technical problems connected with a proposal appeared insoluble or the decision base was inadequate in some other way, or where opinions were divided in the community, the approach was cautious and it might be suggested that a proposal be 'investigated further' or it might be recognized as 'important' without any promise being made for any definite action. It was often stated that things *ought* to be done rather than that they *would* be done. A great many concrete and often minor proposals were included in an appendix, and it was felt that this implied no promises about them. A provisional plan was sent out for comment by everyone who had been involved in making suggestions. As a result a great many oughts were altered to 'will be'. After this the plan was approved by the local section of the party, thus providing the basis for the party's election propaganda. The difference, compared with the other parties, was that a plan was being presented and not just a series of wishes—a plan which would be realized since it had been worked out together with the central party leadership.

The plan then formed the grounds on which a government bill could be based. After making a comprehensive technical examination of the realism, the cost and the possible employment effects of the different suggestions in the plan, the bill was written after barely a month, during which the possibility of implementing some of the measures was further discussed and negotiations were held between technical departments and the Ministry of Finance, and the details of the proposals were worked out. The state-owned enterprise and other organizations in the municipality were given another opportunity to submit demands. A further round of comments from the government departments generated several new suggestions about the arguments which would be used.

The final bill took up a little over half the thirty or so proposals originally included in the plan. It is difficult to say exactly what constitutes a proposal and just how each one was handled, but roughly speaking seven of the proposals were accepted in the bill, albeit often in a somewhat altered form. According to the same kind of assessment, six proposals were referred to new or ongoing investigations. All these proposals were among the more prominent in the plan. But more than half the proposals in the plan were not accepted. Some were rejected explicitly in the bill, but most were simply not mentioned. The proposals that were not mentioned had lacked active advocates either in the government departments or outside them. Nor had they been particularly prominent in the plan.

In presenting the bill, three things in particular were emphasized: that the measures were intended to deal with problems in the short and long term, that the costs amounted to several hundreds of million pounds, and that the bill agreed with the plan. In interviews in the mass media the prime minister emphasized the 'democratic' aspects of the bill: the proposals had been worked out by the residents of the community themselves. Subsequent developments would depend on the people there, and not on centralized decisions in the capital city.

PLACE—IMPLEMENTATION POLICY OR LEGITIMATION POLICY?

How can we interpret the activities described above? To what extent can they be understood in terms of the model presented here: how far can they be interpreted as problem-solving, control, or support?

Problem-Solving

There is nothing to suggest that the work on the PLACE bill had a problem-solving function. Problem-solving would have presupposed an analysis, in which the causes of the problems—in this case the long-term unemployment problem—would have been investigated. The actions to be taken would then have emerged from the analysis. Such an analysis was almost demonstratively avoided; gathering rather than analysis was the method for generating solutions. Furthermore, ideas were sought in the community, that is among those who had demonstrably *not* succeeded in solving the problems themselves. If a start had been made by analysing the problems, there might have been a risk of producing problems without solutions; now, instead, solutions were produced without problems. Nor did the time allowed really permit of any problem-solving: the plan was drawn up in a month and the bill was designed in a couple of months and actually written in a few days.

Nor were the criteria for the gathering of proposals based on any analysis of the problems. Suggestions were rejected or changed because they were too costly, because they did not fit the present aid system, because they came within the brief of committees already sitting, because they largely competed with other communities, or because they were not realistic (e.g. industrial projects which were obviously not profitable). Predictions for future jobs were produced in a slapdash manner.

Nor did any of the actors interviewed claim to know how the problems of the community could be solved. They did not even believe they would be solved, particularly not as a result of the bill. The problems were formulated in terms that were vague or foggy; in the bill the emphasis was on the long-term employment effects while the proposals concerned short-term effects: and when the actors discussed the results of the bill they were more inclined to talk of 'a new spirit' and better profitability in the state-owned enterprise.

Control

All the work on the bill seems incomprehensible if we assume that its function was to solve problems. It is also difficult to interpret it in terms of control, or even as an attempt at control. In presenting the bill the leading politicians emphasized that it was the community's own recommendations that were being supported, not their own. And this was of course absolutely correct, even if the recommendations had two sources. Most suggestions came from the plan, while recommendations for cutbacks in the state-owned company came from the company itself. Even regarding the state-owned company, the express policy was that the political system should not exert control: the company's goal was profitability, and the way this was attained was not a political question but something to be decided by the company board and corporate management.

The central politicians intentionally assumed the role of *defensive examiners* (Brunsson and Jönsson 1979) vis-à-vis proposals from the local politicians and trade unions and civil servants. Instead of taking the initiative themselves, they waited for proposals which they then examined and assessed. It was not the central politicians but the people in the community who took the initiative regarding the development plan. It was not the central politicians who made any suggestions for action; rather, they listened to proposals from the grass-roots. They let themselves be influenced. On this basis they signed a text which contained among other things promises of future action and contributions to be made.

Defensive examiners presuppose suggestion-makers, and such were indeed mobilized. The procedure involved 'soaking up' ideas—all the ideas that were floating about in the party and the trade union could be gathered up in this way. The result was that hardly any ideas that were abroad in the community were left untried. The plan did not contain a single original thought, as one opposition politician declared. But no one had intended that it should.

The 'control' consisted largely of the political system seeing that proposals were put forward, in an area where they wanted—or felt compelled—to do something. That was the function of the plan, and of the plans called for from the state enterprise in the area.

It can be said that it was the central politicians who let themselves be controlled. The central politicians exposed themselves to influence from local actors and from their own civil servants. They limited their own role to saying yes or no to proposals that were actively driven by local politicians or officials. Even the selection of proposals was made in collaboration with the proposers, and as we have seen it mainly followed criteria which had nothing to do with political will. The central politicians simply did not have to make up their minds about any proposals that lacked 'drivers'.

Support for Action

Thus work on the bill had nothing to do with problem-solving and very little with political control. And yet it could still have been implementation-oriented in that it would have supported certain actions which, while not qualifying as problem-solving or having very much to do with political initiative and will, were still intended to be carried out.

However, in the PLACE case there was little need for support for action, since the politicians possessed no problem-solving or control ambitions. Most of the measures had after all been suggested by various groups on the spot, thus enjoying strong support there from the start.

Further the politicians' support for many of the measures was rather vague. Most measures were so cautiously worded that it was not clear whether they were really to be implemented or not: they ought to be carried out, they were 'urgent', or they should be 'investigated further'. Some proposals did not refer to concrete actions, but to some sort of goal. Other proposals were non-operative, for example it was difficult to know exactly what should be done to 'stimulate' or 'support' some particular development. Finally, of course, a whole series of proposals was simply lodged in the appendix to the plan. In the case of a few measures only was any definite promise made.

The measures for which it was difficult to gain acceptance in the community, and which thus needed support if they were to be implemented, were the cutbacks in the state-owned company. These commanded support, but not in the plan. Instead, support and justification were to be found in the company's own plans. The main argument was that like other state-owned companies this one must be run on businesslike lines and must aim to be profitable. Any negative effects should be specially handled. The cutbacks were to be complemented by other positive measures. It is even possible to see the whole bill as compensating—and thus supporting—the reduction in the workforce of the state-owned enterprise. Action there, which could in fact have been suggested by one minister, was supported by the efforts of several ministers and departments.

Direct Political Legitimation

Thus it is rather difficult to find anything in the processes, the arguments or the proposals to suggest that work on the bill was particularly geared to an implementation policy. There are many more factors suggesting that its essential function was directly or indirectly to provide legitimation for the political system. Let us look first at direct ways of legitimizing the political system.

Political organizations create legitimacy for themselves mainly by reflection, that is they seek in some ways to mirror or handle the interests or values of the environment in their organization or their operations. I have already mentioned three main tools for bringing this about: talk, decisions, and action. In working on the bill, the central politicians used all three instruments.

The work was organized in three stages, corresponding to the three instruments. The plan represented the talk level: no decisions were made at that stage. The greater part of the text of the plan is devoted to enumerating the problems of the community and expressing a general wish that action should be looked into, considered, or taken. Every proposal which had some degree of attachment to the community was treated positively in the development plan. In some cases concrete and binding pledges were established. In other cases it was said that measures ought to be carried out, or investigated or considered, and yet other suggestions were assigned to the appendix to the plan—which really meant that the group had decided *not* to support them. All the proposals mentioned were of course already familiar and nobody expected the group to reject them in so many words. Thus the function of the text was not to support action. But nor can it be regarded as providing support for non-action; on the contrary it was emphasized that the community's problems were serious and something must be done to improve the situation. Rather, the function of this part of the process can be seen as a legitimation of the politicians, by reflecting attitudes and values in the relevant environment. The politicians did not say no to the proposals; instead they associated themselves with them, but without binding themselves in any way.

In the bill, which can be said to represent the decision level, the number of proposals had to be reduced: in a decision context any inconsistencies between different proposals become more obvious, and the link with implementation is stronger. The proposals had to be weeded out more severely; those that were loosely anchored in the community, or were subject to differences of opinion, were dropped. Negative decisions were not made unnecessarily; most of the proposals which did not lead to decisions were simply left unmentioned. But the number receiving affirmative decisions was still very high, and some proposals were counted twice. In several cases it was decided to reconsider proposals at some later date in connection with a different investigation.

Because of the time lag between plan and bill, between talking and deciding, it was possible to defend failures of consistency. And in any case, according to the actors, it was never intended that everything in the plan should be decided upon or implemented, particularly those proposals which came into the 'ought to happen' category.

The proposals which were then carried out are the system's actions. And many of the proposals that were agreed upon were in fact realized. But we can also regard some parts of the process as actions. According to the prime minister the process had been democratic since everybody had been able to take part in the process and to influence it. The massive effort in itself should show that the political system cared, and that it was tackling the problems. In a five-line summary on the front page of the bill it was pointed out exactly how much the effort was costing; from a problem-solving point of view, costs should be kept as low as possible, but when it is a question of legitimation the reverse may be true.

The effects of all these legitimizing actions are naturally difficult to pin-point. But many of the actors declared that they provided a high degree of legitimacy. For example, they were believed to have contributed to the party's continuing election successes.

Influencing Responsibility

The main point of the bill was to express the responsibility of the local and central political systems for developments in the community, and the work on the bill was in itself further evidence of this responsibility. However, work on the bill was accompanied by a whole series of arguments indicating that the responsibility of the central politicians and the authorities was not unlimited, particularly not in a future perspective. It was after all proposals emanating from the community and not from the government which were now being decided. It was also firmly pointed out by the central politicians that this was the last time they would take action; after this the residents of the community were to manage on their own—the bill itself was making it possible for them to do so. Just because such vast sums of money were being invested now, the government had no responsibility for the future. In the same way it was pointed out that the state-owned enterprise had now been provided with the conditions needed for profitability; fulfilling the profitability goal was now the responsibility of corporate management, not of the government.

But the inclination to hive off responsibility was not total. In one case the political system decided to assume responsibility, namely when it came to maintaining one profitable state-owned company in the area. If this company had been sold to the municipality, the need for further subsidies would have disappeared altogether. But that proposal was rejected already before the plan was written. Perhaps this community and its problems provided an important arena for the political system, which the central politicians did not want to lose altogether?

Influencing the Legitimacy of the Situation

Some features in the process, the proposals, and the arguments were functional for making the community feel more satisfied with its situation. The bill undeniably demonstrated that, despite the severity of the problems, the government was doing everything it possibly could. No suggestions that could be regarded as technically possible and that enjoyed widespread support in the community were actually rejected. Somebody cared, somebody wanted to help. The political system also tried to arouse expectations that things would be better in the future and the problems might perhaps be solved. This openly expressed belief in the future was in marked contrast to the great pessimism among the central politicians themselves as to whether the problems could ever really be solved.

Most of the politicians interviewed emphasized the importance of the policy in legitimizing the situation. When they were asked about the possible future effects of the bill, they said that certain effects could already be noted: they had enhanced people's way of thinking about and facing up to their situation although no concrete action had been taken as yet. The great importance of the plan and the bill was that a new spirit had arisen in the community, people had come to believe in the future with optimism, courage, self-esteem, and determination. The 'depression' and pessimism which had formerly prevailed was the main reason for composing the plan and the bill at all.

Giving legitimacy to the prevailing situation must have been an important task, in view of the predictions which the politicians actually made. Not one of them believed that the concrete problems of the community would really be resolved, despite the measures which were to be adopted. They did not expect the unemployment figures to fall; they believed they would remain the highest in the country.

If the impact on feelings in the community was really as great as the politicians claimed, it was quite remarkable: during the period when this change of heart was talking place, unemployment in the area actually increased as a result of cutbacks in the state-owned company.

A SUMMARY

The result of the analysis is not particularly surprising. The process, the proposals, and the arguments are all incomprehensible if we assume that their function was implementation in the sense of problem-solving and control. What actually happened has little in common with the picture conjured up by the implementation model, with the politicians trying to impose their ideas about what should be done on to a refractory environment. The whole thing becomes comprehensible only if we assume that support and legitimation were the prime goals. That the politicians had no problem-solving function is not surprising, since none of them had any idea how the community's problems could be solved and since they did not even believe that they could be solved. Perhaps it was just because the problem really was insoluble, that the politicians felt they ought or had to intervene. And since it was not possible to devote themselves to solving the problems, they naturally had little interest in exerting control either, restricting themselves mainly to what was feasible and desirable in the situation as it was, namely supporting the 'necessary' cutbacks in the state-owned company and legitimizing the political system and the situation in the community.

The politicians' main function here was legitimation. And this also seems to have been what they intended and what they achieved. Nothing suggests that the process was irrational, that is that the actors were being forced into the various steps against their will or their sense of what was appropriate.

The Role of Politics

The PLACE case provides an illustration of the role of the state as legitimator: legitimizing both itself and its environment. Naturally the case does not reveal legitimation as the state's only function. But it does show that we cannot always assume the state to be aiming at implementation—solving problems, exerting control, or transforming decisions into action. The hierarchic metaphor is misleading not only in the cases described here, but in several other studies of state and political control as well (Swedish examples are Brunsson and Rombach 1982; Brunsson and Jönsson 1979; Olson 1983; Jacobsson 1984; Wiberg 1985). The political system, like the state as a whole, finds it difficult to control its environment; and as well as its environment it is concerned with its own position. Influencing the environment need not necessarily involve control; instead it can involve legitimation.

The fact that it is popular to talk about implementation, about the political system solving problems and exerting control, need not have much connection with things as they are. Rather, it may reflect myths about organizations—myths which are in fact extremely functional. Paradoxically, political organizations often try to establish their legitimacy by proclaiming their focus on problems and action and their lack of interest in their own legitimacy. Action is important, and action is motivated by problems (cf. Starbuck 1983).

Industrial policy is obviously an area in which implementation is very difficult, a rational political system can be expected to avoid as far as possible a policy of implementation. Too little is known about the identity of the problems, their interconnectedness, causes, and possible solutions, to provide any basis for rational—as opposed to superstitious—problem-solving. It is difficult to know what industrial development would be appropriate. How, for example, should we balance an interest in job opportunities against an interest in a high level of technology? Nobody knows what causes industrial development, and we know even less about how political systems can stimulate it. Controlling industrial companies and steering their development is no easy matter. And this being so, it does not seem particularly rational to put the main emphasis on problem-solving and control. Rather, we should expect industrial policy to include a significant element of legitimation. A policy geared to making people 'happier', to 'increasing their welfare' or to 'promoting their interests' for example, can be expected to contain a large measure of responsibility-assumption, in other words of legitimation strategy.

A high degree of legitimacy in the political system and in the situation is probably also important to the stability of the system. Attempts on the part of the political system to steer industry in a particular direction will have a destabilizing effect, while also reducing the political system's ability to reflect a variety of interests and values. This in turn makes it more difficult for it to create legitimacy in this way. Legitimacy then has to be based on action instead, that is on implementing actions that satisfy diverse interests and views. But if there is doubt about the efficacy of the actions of the politicians in this respect, then legitimation by reflection is better for the political system. Perhaps it is also better for the industrial system and the citizens.

Perhaps the role of politics in society often involves something far more important than controlling and redistributing material resources. Its task is perhaps rather to create well-being and happiness, in other words to exert an influence on ideology, and it may not always be necessary to proceed the long way via controlling material resources. In the PLACE case, for example, the politicians felt that the major effects arose from their talk and decisions, not from actions undertaken by the state.

A given situation can be legitimized by affecting the way people think about it. But it can also be legitimized by the assumption of responsibility. Man has a strong desire to explain events, both the good and the bad (Geertz 1973). In a secularized culture such as our own, it is important to be able to explain things by reference to people: if people rather than chance or natural forces or social laws have caused an event, this also means that the event can be controlled. An illusion of explanation and control can help to reduce existential anxiety (van Gunsteren 1976). Since assuming responsibility is to establish oneself as a cause of what has happened, one way of assuming responsibility is to make decisions. Decisions suggest a choice between alternatives, and in choosing a particular action you become at least part of its cause.

The political system sets great store by decisions, and politicians often claim openly to have influenced decisions. Furthermore, they can make decisions about almost anything, not only the government's actions but also those of the citizens or of business firms. Politicians readily assume responsibility or have it assigned to them. For the people around them it is perhaps particularly important that they assume responsibility for situations perceived as negative or troublesome. That someone should bear the burden of our sins has been a central tenet of Western Christian culture for almost 2,000 years, and we can therefore assume that the idea will persist even if the sins are now borne by another. From this point of view our regular carping at the politicians and our criticisms of the state and its institutions in periods of economic decline, are something quite natural and serving a necessary function. Politics and the politicians are more important, more crucial, to our culture than the hierarchic metaphor implies.

Assuming responsibility and creating legitimacy are important political tasks. The way they are effected is by making decisions and claiming to exert control. But the means should not be unreflectingly interpreted as goals.

REFERENCES

Brunsson, N. (1983). *Projektinstitutionalisering—ett fall.* Stockholm: EFI.

_____ (1985). *The Irrational Organization.* Chichester, UK: Wiley.

_____ and Jönsson, S. (1979). *Beslut och handling.* Stockholm: Liber.

_____ and Rombach, B. (1982). *Går det att spara?* Lund, Sweden: Doxa.

Gandemo, B. (1983). *Investeringar i företag.* Stockholm: SIND.

Geertz. C. (1973). *The Interpretation of Cultures.* New York: Basic Books.

van Gunsteren, H. (1976). *The Quest for Control.* London: Wiley.

Jacobsson, B. (1984). *Hur styrs förvaltningen?* Lund, Sweden: Studentlitteratur.

Olson, O. (1983). *Ansvar och ändamål.* Lund, Sweden: Doxa.

Starbuck, W. (1983). 'Organizations as Action Generator', *American Sociological Review*, 48: 91–102.

Swedish Government Official Report (1981). Att avveckla en kortsiktig stödpolitik. Stockholm.

Wiberg, S. (1985). Bild och handling. Manuscript. Göteborg.

7

Organized Hypocrisy

The secret of success is honesty and fair dealing. If you can fake those, you've got it made.

Groucho Marx

For a number of years, the European Union was criticized for the high and unfair customs rate it has charged on bananas imported from countries other than the former European colonies. In 2001, the EU decided to harmonize customs duties for all exporting countries—within five years.

The intensity of car traffic within the city of Stockholm has long been a controversial issue. Traffic increased in Stockholm during the 1990s but city officials could refer to the decision they made at the beginning of the decade to reduce traffic by 30 per cent in fifteen years.

When the Swedish corporation, Ericsson, moved part of its head offices to London, large promotional posters appeared in Swedish cities depicting an enormous Swedish flag with Ericsson as the sender.

HYPOCRISY REVISITED

The introductory examples describe statements from various organizations—they are examples of how organizations talk. In the first two examples, the organizations presented what they called decisions. Decisions can be seen as a special type of talk that indicates a will to act and a choice of action. In traditional decision theory, a decision is taken to be indicative of a corresponding action that will occur in the future, or at least the decision is assumed to increase the probability of such an action. Organizational management teams—governments, corporate leaders, or the board of an association, for example—often use decisions in their attempts to govern the actions of other organization members.

There is also talk without decisions. Management presents visions, business concepts, objectives, policies, or political programmes that are not decisions regarding specific actions but aimed at convincing members of the organization to act in accordance with management talk. According to traditional administrative wisdom, this kind of talk is expected to have the same effect as decisions—it is assumed to increase the probability for corresponding action. Talk may also affect actions indirectly: talk along a certain vein leads to decisions with the same content, which lead, in turn, to the corresponding action.

In practice, it is not always the case that traditional theory and wisdom reflect realities. There are not always strong connections among talk, decisions, and actions—neither for individuals nor for organizations. To talk is one thing; to decide is a second; to act is yet a third. People talk, decide, and act on separate occasions and in different contexts; and some people talk and decide about how others should act. It is possible to act without making a decision or talking about it, and it is possible to talk and decide without actually acting on it. So there is reason to suspect that there will often be discrepancies among what is said, what is decided, and what is done.

As the examples demonstrate, it is also possible to act contrary to what one has said or decided. People may talk or decide about a certain action but act in the opposite way. The result is hypocrisy.[1] According to the Oxford Dictionary[2] hypocrisy means 'the assumption or postulation of moral standards to which one's own behaviour does not conform'. This definition contains the same distinction that I have made here regarding what is said and what is done, as well as the idea that what is said and done can have varying degrees of correspondence. The definition being used in this chapter is, however, somewhat broader than that of the dictionary: it also encompasses talk, decisions, and actions related to things outside the 'moral' realm. Thus it is not necessarily the case that what is said is better than what is done. Instead, it may be true that some people believe that what is said is right, others believe that what is decided is right, and still others believe that what is actually done is right. Thereby, hypocrisy can satisfy a variety of different interests, as explained below.

Hypocrisy is a concept tied to an 'actor': only actors can be hypocritical. There are two types of actors in modern society: individuals and organizations.[3] In Western culture actors are assumed to be bounded, coherent, coordinated, and sovereign entities with intentions, who are able to talk, decide, and act, and who control their own actions.

Hypocrisy is a kind of inconsistency within an actor. Inconsistencies *among* actors in society are generally seen as routine and are not necessarily perceived

---

[1] N. Brunsson (1986, 1995, 2002).

[2] *The Concise Oxford Dictionary of Current English* (1995).

[3] Meyer et al. (1987).

to be problematic. Inconsistencies *within* actors, however, seem less ordinary and more problematic. The general norm is that actors should be consistent in what they say, decide, and do. Hypocrisy is usually deemed to be a problem. For instance, it is common to talk about 'implementation problems' in organizations when the organization does not execute the visions stated or the decisions made. Hypocrisy even challenges moral norms. At first blush, a hypocrite is assumed to be acting in a morally indefensible way. However, these ideas about hypocrisy are open to debate. As I discuss later, hypocrisy is not necessarily a problem; sometimes it can be a solution. And hypocrisy can be seen as morally valuable, at least compared to its options.

In order to explain hypocrisy in the organizational realm, we need a model with two basic assumptions: one regarding conflict, and one regarding the output of organizations.

Conflict

Hypocrisy is a response to a world in which values, ideas, or people are in conflict—a way in which individuals and organizations handle such conflicts. Organizations are routinely exposed to conflict. People have different and often contradictory ideas about how an organization should work and what it should achieve, and to satisfy one demand fully may be to satisfy poorly or to fail to satisfy another.[4] Modern organizations are particularly apt to pretend that they can satisfy a series of conflicting demands. Sometimes they seem to do so as a response to external or internal pressures, sometimes managements seem to actively and voluntary make such pretences.

For example, modern companies should not only be profitable. They should provide employment; offer a good working environment that provides opportunities for personal development; provide their employees with decent wages; give good service to their customers; contribute to the prosperity, GDP, export revenue, and the general progression of the countries in which they are active—while not polluting the environment. Modern states should help families and senior citizens, domestic farmers, and the economies of developing countries; they should have low taxes and expensive welfare programmes, offer a good working environment for their police forces and provide police service twenty-four hours a day and seven days a week. As positive as these demands are, it is not easy for a company or state to satisfy them all. Success in one dimension often decreases success in another.

Conflict occurs among groups: different groups of people demand different things. Conflict occurs over time: the same people can have different demands

[4] Friedlander and Pickle (1968).

at different times. And conflict occurs within individuals because individuals occupy different roles, which include different opinions and interests, some of which are contradictory, and it is not a given that individuals have an order of preference for weighing values against each other.[5] Truthfully, wouldn't we all like to have companies and states that lived up to all the demands mentioned above?

Also, there are conflicts or tensions between ideology and practice. In modern society there are many popular ideas of what is generally rational, just, or good. Such ideas tend to be general, vague, and simple, making them attractive as ideas[6] but more difficult to translate into concrete, specific actions in a way that is as attractive and uncontroversial as the ideas.[7] Organizations are systems that are supposed to act, so for them the tension between attractive ideas and the limits and specificities of practice becomes acute. They are easy victims for the criticism of having perverted our ideals. Modern organizations are squeezed between ideology and practice.

Talk as Output

Hypocrisy is meaningful only if talk and decisions have an intrinsic value. A central but often implicit assumption in traditional decision theory is that action is the focal point of interest, and that talk and decisions have no value or interest per se; their only value is in paving the road to a predicated action. But this assumption does not seem to fit modern organizations.

It seems that in practice, there is strong interest not only in the actions of organizations but also in what they say and decide—even in organizations that also produce concrete products. Organizations are surrounded not only by consumers but also by audiences. Modern organizations produce a great deal of talk and decisions. Organizations are seldom secretive about their visions, programmes, and important decisions; on the contrary, these are often published. Modern corporations have communication departments that specialize in explaining the what and why of current strategies and decisions to external and internal parties. Parliaments of all kinds are conscientious about public debates and well-publicized decisions. Indeed, politics in general revolves, to a large extent, around ways of talking and of presenting decisions.[8] And organizations rarely need to go begging for attention—mass media interest is high for organizational planning, strategies, programmes, opinions, and decisions. Thus, talk and decision seem to have value as a kind of output created by organizations. It appears that organizations are

---

[5] Veyne (1983); Loewenstein and Elster (1992).   [6] Strang and Meyer (1993).
[7] Sartori (1962).   [8] Edelman (1964).

often valued not merely for their actions but also for what they say and the decisions they make. Publicity is often as important as, if not more, than the product.

Talk and Decision as Compensation

If we assume that talk and decisions are valued outputs of organizations and that organizations are subject to conflicting demands, we will have the ingredients for a model in which the connections among what is said, decided, and done is different from what is often expected. If people who place demands on an organization attach importance not only to the organization's actions but also to what is said and decided, the organization can meet some demands through talk, others through its decisions, and yet others through action—and thus to some extent satisfy three conflicting demands. Or, contrariwise, in this situation it becomes difficult to act consistently with what is said and what is decided. To do so would be to satisfy one interest while leaving the others completely unsatisfied. It would be easier to act in one direction if either the talk or the decision indicates the opposite. In this model, the likelihood of an action decreases the more it is talked about and the more clear decisions are made about it. Its likelihood increases if what is said and decided is in opposition to it. Talk and decisions in one direction *compensate for* actions in the opposite direction and vice versa. Hypocrisy is a way of handling conflicts by reflecting them in inconsistencies among talk, decisions, and actions.

The model of hypocrisy can be applied to the examples at the beginning of this chapter. According to the model, the decision to lift the ban on bananas within five years is the decisive *precondition* for the action to continue preventing banana imports through the use of high customs rates. If the decision had not been contradictory to the action, it would have been difficult to continue with the action. The protests against the high customs duties would probably have become too strong. The decision to decrease traffic in Stockholm made it easier to gain acceptance for the fact that it was actually increasing; it weakened the arguments of those who opposed the increasing traffic because, after all, the decision had been made to decrease traffic—eventually. And Ericsson would not need to put money into a campaign advertising its Swedishness if it were not moving its head offices abroad.

The model of hypocrisy challenges traditional decision theory and administrative wisdom. According to traditional theory talk, decisions, and actions are causally related in a special way: talk or decisions aimed in one direction increase the likelihood of the corresponding action. In the model of hypocrisy talk, decisions, and actions are still causally related, but the causality is the reverse: talk or decisions in one direction decrease the likelihood of corresponding actions, and actions in one direction decrease the likelihood of corresponding talk and decisions. The model of hypocrisy implies that talk, decisions, and actions are 'coupled' rather than 'de-coupled'[9] or 'loosely coupled',[10] but they are coupled in a way other than usually assumed.

It is not a coincidence that I discovered a great deal of hypocrisy when I researched Swedish municipalities. Swedish municipalities are highly autonomous units; they are truly actors, in contrast to many other European municipal systems that are strongly subordinated to national governments. Swedish municipalities are similar to nation states, and just like states they are subject to strongly conflicting demands. Along with states this type of municipality is less able than most other organizations to avoid conflicts in their environments—conflicts among differing interests as well as inconsistencies between ideology and practice. Moreover, it is integral to them that they are able to deal with conflicts that cannot be dealt with elsewhere, and that they are structured to facilitate this task.[11] They produce a great deal of talk and decisions. For local and central governments that must handle highly controversial issues, it is often easier to act contrary to the ways in which they talk, and wise to talk contrary to the ways in which they act. So it is no surprise that it is often easier for liberal governments to socialize and for socialist governments to privatize,[12] or that increases in trade barriers are combined with much presidential talk about the benefits of free trade (as in the case of the introduction of US steel customs at the time of writing).[13]

Within this model, hypocrisy gains a functional meaning. The differences among that which is said, that which is decided, and that which is done do not constitute the problems implied by traditional decision theory. There is still a lack of implementation, but no implementation *problem*. Instead, hypocrisy is a solution—a solution to several problems. Hypocrisy makes it easier to act forcefully in one direction, even with a number of opponents. It also becomes easier to say controversial things and to make controversial decisions.

Hypocrisy also makes it easier to maintain the legitimacy of organizations, even when they are subjected to conflicting demands. There can be more parties that are at least moderately satisfied with the organization than there would be without hypocrisy. Without hypocrisy, one party or interest would be completely satisfied and all others completely dissatisfied. With hypocrisy, several parties and interests can be somewhat satisfied. Those who are against

[9] Meyer and Rowan (1977).   [10] Weick (1976).   [11] N. Brunsson (2002).
[12] Garme (2001).   [13] Whitehouse News Release (20020305-6).

a high customs rate on bananas may be dissatisfied that such rates exist, but they will be somewhat solaced by the fact that a decision has been made to reduce the rates. Those who want a high customs rate may be concerned about the decision, but they can take solace in the fact that high rates are actually charged. Neither party has their needs fully met, but neither is anyone left completely unsatisfied.

An organization that could not deal in hypocrisy would have a more difficult time working in a world of conflicts than will one that can. Similarly, it can be assumed that conflict situations are generally easier to accept if the response can be hypocritical. In a world without hypocrisy, strong dissatisfaction would probably be more common, suggesting that hypocrisy is a solution for those who want to promote happiness and social stability.

In the remainder of the chapter, I discuss more detailed aspects of talk, conflict, and hypocrisy. First I expand the theme of talk and decisions as output, which further explains why hypocrisy has an effect. Then I discuss conflict in a more detailed way, which will contribute to an understanding of the reasons why hypocrisy arises in organizations. In later sections I analyse the phenomenon of 'meta-hypocrisy' as well as the stability of hypocrisy. Finally, I draw some normative conclusions.

TALK AS OUTPUT—HOW HYPOCRISY WORKS

As mentioned above, in order for hypocrisy to work, it is necessary that there are people who attach importance not only to what organizations do but also to what they say and the decisions they make. People find talk and decisions important for various reasons. Some people may think that talk and decisions are important in and of themselves. To perceive the ideas that organizations represent as important and to believe that it is important for organizations to speak of high morals even in the face of a harsh reality seems to be a highly respectable position. These 'idealists' will be open to hypocrisy because they consider their interests and values to be at least partially satisfied through what is said and decided.

But perhaps more common in contemporary Western culture is the opposite opinion: that organizations exist in order to achieve, and it is their actions that are really important. At first blush it appears that the 'materialists' who hold this view should attach no importance to what is said and decided. But whether they actually do or not depends on which theory they embrace regarding the connection among talk, decision, and action. If they do not believe that such a connection exists, they will attach no importance to talk and decision. If they do believe there are connections among the three, however, the situation is different. If the materialists adhere to the tenets of traditional administrative and decision theories, which assume positive causal relationships among talk, decision, and action, they will attach importance to what is said and done because they believe that talk and decisions in one direction will increase the likelihood of the corresponding action—their ultimate interest.

Considering the pervasiveness of traditional theories, there is reason to believe that many materialists believe in them. They may be people within the organization who set goals or make decisions because they want the corresponding action to be achieved; or they may be people external to the organization who pay careful attention to goals, other statements, or decisions in order to predict future actions. All of these people pay attention to what is said and to what decisions are made and can, therefore, be influenced by hypocrisy.

For these materialists, the theory of hypocrisy will apply precisely because they do not believe in it. For the materialist who does not believe in traditional theory, but believes instead in the theory of hypocrisy, hypocrisy will not work. If everyone was a materialist and believed in the model of hypocrisy described here, this model would no longer be valid. Then people would attach importance to what was said and what was decided, but would fear that the talk and the decisions would actually prevent the corresponding action from being implemented. Thus actions could not be compensated for by talk and decisions, and the likelihood of a certain action would no longer increase if the opposite action was talked about and decided upon.

For example, for the materialistic environmentalist believing in traditional theory, talk and decisions about improving the environment are good things that somewhat compensate for the fact that there is current pollution; they are signs that the environment will improve in the future. For environmentalists who believe in the theory of hypocrisy, talk and decisions about improving the environment would be signs that future actions would have a negative impact on the environment. Such talk and decisions would therefore increase their dissatisfaction and alert their opposition. In this case, talk and decisions about being environmentally friendly would decrease the possibility of implementing environmentally disruptive actions, rather than the other way around. Hypocrisy for materialists is one example of the fact that certain effects are realized in a social system only when people believe in other effects.

Ambiguity

A further complication can arise as a result of ambiguity as to the real nature of talk, decisions, and actions. The hypocrisy model is based on the ability to distinguish among these three. It is common to make the distinction between words and deeds. To talk about something is usually seen as being quite different from doing it. In daily life, people usually have no problem distinguishing between talk and actions, even if the distinction easily becomes problematic from a more philosophical point of view.[14] This is one of many examples of a tendency in our daily lives to solve a series of philosophical and theoretical problems that would be rendered difficult if we thought about them more closely. Sometimes, however, the distinction becomes difficult not only upon greater reflection but also in daily life.

There are organizations that have difficulty acting at all. They are 'others' rather than actors.[15] Rather than acting themselves, they criticize actors, make rules for them, or give them advice. Organizational consultants, for instance, seem to produce only talk or 'to deal in words'.[16] If there are no actions, there can, by definition, be no hypocrisy.

Talk and decisions generally reach wider audiences than actions do.[17] Few people have much knowledge about organizational actions, for actions are usually more private and not as easy to gain knowledge about as are talk and decisions. So many people may perceive talk and decision as being equivalent to action. Typically, only a relatively small number of people are affected by pollution, are direct customers of a company or work for it, or have customs imposed on them. Only those few people will actually be able to experience the action. The rest are spectators, who have no first-hand knowledge of the action; at most, their 'knowledge' is hearsay. One way of discovering the action is to listen to how it is described in organizational talk and decisions. If these descriptions have little competition from other descriptions, they easily form our ideas about the action.

In cases where the spectators and those who are directly affected by the actions have different interests, confusion of talk, decisions, and actions facilitates hypocrisy: talk and decisions can be adapted to the interests of the spectators and action to the interests of those involved. In 1987, following harsh criticism, the Swedish government decided to prohibit the housing of hens in small cages, a practice considered reprehensible by animal rights activists but deemed to be the most economical by egg producers. The decision received a great deal of attention, and was described as an eightieth birthday present for the famous author and pioneer animal right activist Astrid Lindgren. But because a subordinate governmental agency continually granted exceptions, the majority of Swedish hens still were living in their old cages when Ms Lindgren died at the age of 95. If the people who support better treatment of hens are primarily spectators, and the people who have a financial interest

---

[14] Austin (1962).   [15] Meyer (1996).   [16] Czarniawska-Joerges (1990).

[17] As already noted by Machiavelli (1513), ch. XVIII: 'Everyone sees what you appear to be, few experience what you really are.'

in hens are those who are actually affected by the action, then both interests can be satisfied in this manner. In such cases, it is in the interests of the organization to create and support the spectators' impression that talk and decisions are accurate descriptions of actions. If they are successful, everyone is happy (except the hens, perhaps).

In other instances, an organization's talk and decisions can influence the image of its actions even for those who are directly affected by the latter. Those involved—customers, for example—often experience only a limited, specialized part of all the organization's actions. As for other organizational actions they, as much as anyone else, are spectators who are readily influenced by the organization's description of its actions. Even if they are dissatisfied with the actions that affect them, it does not necessarily follow that they are dissatisfied with the actions of the organization in general. If their contact with the actions of the organization is infrequent, they may be convinced by the organization's talk and decisions that their own experience is exceptional.

For example, if one is rarely a patient within the health care system, it is possible to believe that one's experience of poor service is exceptional, particularly if the organization responsible for that care has set goals and made forceful decisions to become service oriented. This exception is indeed negative, but it is difficult to use it to condemn all health care provided by the organization. It is, after all, hardly advisable to draw conclusions based solely on one's own limited experience. In this example, the organization could satisfy the interest in service by presenting itself as service oriented and by making decisions to be service oriented, while simultaneously satisfying financial interests by not having the staff or spending the funds necessary to offer that service in practice. In a state-financed health care system this would mean that the tax-payers would be reasonably satisfied with both the service offered and its cost.

CONFLICTING DEMANDS—HOW HYPOCRISY ARISES

The fact that hypocrisy can have a functional value may lead one to suspect that it is sometimes used as a conscious strategy by certain actors in situations of conflicting demands—by managers, for example, or by others for whom the legitimacy of an organization is important. But organizational hypocrisy also arises without anyone having intended it. Hypocrisy is not merely an active answer to conflict; it also arises as a result of conflict.

The proponents of one demand within or outside an organization can actively attempt to prevent the fulfilment of other demands, because the realization of other demands decreases the likelihood that their demand is satisfied. A decision about a certain action can be the very impetus for the opponents to make active resistance that prevents the implementation of the action. Simultaneously, the decision tends to pacify those who favour the decided action and cause them to be less anxiously engaged in ensuring that the decision is actually implemented. The effect is a difference in decision and action. For example, local resistance against a planned road tends to become strongest after the decision to build the road has been made. The decision awakens the opposition, which, if sufficiently strong, can prevent the implementation of the decision. The result is organizational hypocrisy.

Conflicting demands imply that there is always someone to question what the organization is doing. It is not unusual to set goals in areas where the organization is weak, in areas in which it has not succeeded in satisfying a certain interest through action. Such goals are, by definition, examples of hypocrisy, for they express what is not being done. For companies that create a great deal of pollution, it is more important than for others to have environmental goals. Setting goals can be called a conscious strategy that leads to hypocrisy but the goal-setters may in fact intend eventually to abolish the differences among talk, decision, and action. In other words, the purpose is the opposite of hypocrisy.

Hypocrisy is one of many ways of handling conflicts among groups. The incentive and opportunity for hypocrisy diminish when there are other ways out. One way of handling conflicts is to let one view predominate. There can, for example, be rules that give the majority the right to enforce its view—a tenable solution if there is broad acceptance for the principle that determines predominance. Another solution is to compromise, to satisfy several points of view partially but none fully. A third solution is 'logrolling' whereby group A supports an alternative that they do not like but that is preferred by group B—in exchange for group B's support for group A's favourite alternative in another issue. A fourth solution is to satisfy different interests at different times, that is, what Cyert and March[18] called 'sequential attention to goals'.

It is often implied in conflict theories that conflicts are associated with action and that the different parties will be satisfied only by actions. But these theories can be applied to talk and decisions as well. As long as people care about what is said and what is decided upon, their interests can be met through talk and decisions based on predominance, compromise, logrolling, or sequential attention to goals.

But if talk and decisions are relevant, they also point to a further way of resolving conflict—namely to satisfy all interests simultaneously by either talk

---

[18] Cyert and March (1963).

or decisions. As argued above, it is often easier and less expensive to satisfy conflicting demands with talk and decision-making than it is by actions, and it is possible even when the corresponding contradictory actions are impossible to carry out simultaneously. A parliamentary debate comprises a multitude of opinions, and most of the opinions on any given issue are usually dealt with in this manner. Similarly, it is possible to make decisions that represent conflicting opinions. So inconsistent talk and decisions can, therefore, satisfy conflicting demands; they are instances of double talk, but they are not, in themselves, instances of hypocrisy. But in an organization that does not merely talk but also acts, contradictory talk and decisions will tend to lead to some hypocrisy, because it is difficult to act according to all talk and decisions if these are contradictory.

The probability of hypocrisy is increased when the other ways of handling conflicts do not work. The option to choose to satisfy only one demand can be nullified by the fact that acceptance of the principle of dominance is low because, for example, it is not seen as acceptable that the majority win out over the minority. Logrolling is difficult to use when people are not willing to give up their positions completely in certain issues. Compromise in talk and in decision-making is often relatively easy to achieve, but compromise is more difficult to achieve in action, in particular when some people are demanding that the organization should act in a certain way and others are demanding that it should not. Sequential attention to goals does not impress parties with short-time horizons for their demands. Also, sequential attention to goals can counteract demands on efficiency: it can lead to a great deal of inefficiency if things are done that counteract some earlier action. Finally, handling conflicts merely by talking and making decisions is difficult if everyone agrees that the organization should produce some action.

Conflict Over Time

Conflicts may occur across time, so different demands are made on the organization at different times. Sometimes such demands change more rapidly than the organization is able to act. If we want action, such demands can be handled only if we allow for hypocrisy: the organization adapts its talk and decisions quickly enough to reflect new demands, but not slowly enough to reflect its actions.

Fashions provide one example of quickly changing demands. When fashions change more rapidly than the organization is able to act, hypocrisy will easily arise. For example, the fashions concerning management techniques seem often to change more quickly than the time it takes to implement these techniques. In such situations, it is impossible to act according to the model currently in fashion. But it is easier to adapt talk and decisions at a pace that keeps abreast of fashion changes. Talk and decisions can then be adapted to the fashion, but only on the condition that they need not reflect action—that is under conditions of hypocrisy. The organization is left to work according to an old model, while always being seen to have made the decision to implement the latest fashion. It would not be meaningful to implement the new fashions because they would be obsolete before the implementation process was complete. An organization that was not allowed to be hypocritical and had to adapt what it said and what was decided to what it actually did would appear hopelessly old fashioned (unless it succeeded in divining some future fashion and adopted it just before it actually became fashionable). And needless to say there are other fashions and other demands on an organization that can change quickly over time, giving rise to a similar situation and to hypocrisy.

What Can Be Said and What Can Be Done

A further factor that leads to hypocrisy is the tension between ideology and practice. Talk and decisions follow rules for what can be said, actions follow rules for what can be done, and we cannot expect that these rules will always be consistent. There are things that we can say but not do, and there are other things that we can do but not say.[19] This situation easily leads to hypocrisy.

First, let us consider the fact that there are many things we can say but are difficult to translate into action for a variety of reasons. Talk and decisions are often less expensive than actions. Even when the decision is easy, we may not have sufficient knowledge, resources, time, or power to implement an action. And it is easy to talk and to make decisions that are contradictory, but to act in a conflicting manner demands greater resources and is the opposite of effective. It is not difficult to speak well of both profitability and a good working environment, or to decide to increase government subsidies to families with children and to senior citizens. But to implement all the corresponding actions tends to be a harder task.

Nor is it guaranteed that the actions about which people talk and decide are at all possible to implement. Good ideas are the easiest ones to agree upon, but what people think are good ideas are often those that express what is beautiful, true, and just rather than what is realistic, pragmatic, and feasible. And people may talk about or decide to both to act and not to act in a certain way, but to implement such talk and decisions is impossible.

[19] N. Brunsson (1995).

There are also things that we can do but not say. What one can say is often limited more stringently than what one can do by rules relating to aesthetics, ethics, and truth, by perceptions of how things should be and how things are. People may perform immoral acts without much difficulty, but it is more difficult to acknowledge such actions. It is even more difficult to proclaim one's own decision to be immoral—to state, in effect, that one wants to be immoral.

Similarly, when we talk about something, we often need to refer to that which our audience believes to be true in order for us to sound credible or even to be understood. But what one believes to be true can have but a tenuous tie to what one does. The official truth about institutions can deviate substantially from the ways in which these institutions actually operate.[20] For example, the truth about organizations is very closely tied to the concept of rationality. Most management teams, therefore, present their organizations as rational systems in which the actions of the organization are the product of rational deliberations. Furthermore, it is difficult to decide that the organization should not be rational. If we are to believe four decades of research on organizations, however, the operation of most organizations is far from being characterized by fully rational behaviour. Thus organizations can talk about rationality and decide to become more rational without this actually affecting its actions. Decisions to implement rational control systems often fail.[21]

Hypocrisy is a way of handling situations when what is said cannot be done and when what is done cannot be talked about. Hypocrisy means that we can continue to talk about things that can be talked about and do things that can be done. What can be said is not limited by what can be done, and vice versa.

META-HYPOCRISY

As argued above, the idea that talk, decisions, and actions should be consistent is not merely a common assumption but also a widespread norm in society for those who are seen as actors: neither individuals nor organizations should engage in hypocrisy. What they say, what they decide, and what they do should be in agreement. If actors can be proven to be hypocrites, they can be censured according to this norm.

In a worst-case scenario, the criticism could not only censure them but also discredit them as actors. An organization can, for example, be accused of not really being a coordinated unit. Its hypocrisy is taken as proof that the organization is not actually one actor, but consists of many independent and uncoordinated individuals or departments each being an actor on its own.

---

[20] Arnold (1937).
[21] Wildavsky (1975); Rombach (1991); and Holmblad Brunsson (2002).

It is not only morale and belief in actorhood that are jeopardized by allegations that a person or organization is hypocritical, but also the actual results of hypocrisy. If people do not believe that an organization is one actor, faith is undermined in the positive causal relations among what is said, decided, and done. If talk, decisions, and actions are perceived as being performed by different actors, the expectation for consistency is not as strong as when one actor is in charge of all three steps. So there is a risk that 'materialists' with this belief will not pay attention to talk and decisions. Also, as mentioned previously, hypocrisy works for the materialists only if they do not believe in hypocrisy. It is, therefore, important to convince materialists that the organization is one actor and that there is no hypocrisy—that the only function of talk and decisions is to create the corresponding action. Doing that is in itself a form of hypocrisy, but on a higher level—a 'meta-hypocrisy'—the posture that a hypocritical organization is not a hypocrite. Meta-hypocrisy is a crucial factor in the success of the underlying hypocrisy. The more important as independent outputs are talk and decisions, the more important it is to emphasize that the only important thing is what is actually done, and that talk and decisions are only preparatory to action.

Meta-hypocrisy can be understood in a way similar to the basic hypocrisy. The norm that makes hypocrisy unacceptable is another demand on individuals and on organizations that is above and beyond all other demands placed on them. If the other demands are contradictory, sometimes the only solution is hypocrisy. The demand that one should not be a hypocrite is contradictory to the sum of the other demands: one should not be hypocritical plus one should be hypocritical. This contradictory demand can be met with hypocrisy in the same way that hypocrisy is used to meet other contradictory demands, but it raises hypocrisy to the level of meta-hypocrisy: one continues to be a hypocrite but one claims that one is not. The organization is presented as being consistent with regards to what is said, decided, and done, but in practice this is not always the case.

The less consistency there is in talk, decision, and action, the more likely is that there will be an accusation of hypocrisy, and the more important it is to assert that there is no hypocrisy. This situation leads to forceful attempts to describe the organization as one coherent actor in which the visions of management are indeed not merely talk but permeate all actions, where actions are fundamental, and where talk and decisions have as their sole purpose to create action. In my experience, this type of description is not uncommon when companies are described by their managements.

Just as in the case of the basic form of hypocrisy, a time aspect can be applied to meta-hypocrisy. This is especially important when it is difficult to assert that the past and present are not characterized by hypocrisy. The argument then becomes that talk, decisions, and actions will be connected in an organization in the long term, even if this has not been successful in the past. The organization will be changed so that it comes more in line with the actor concept, with greater coherence and control. That is the theme in much organizational reform.[22]

STABLE AND UNSTABLE HYPOCRISY

Hypocrisy may be a more or less stable phenomenon—it may persist or it may disappear over time. The stability of hypocrisy is threatened by tendencies towards implementation, tendencies towards justification, and by the norm of consistency.

Implementation

Hypocrisy tends to create much future. In several of the examples above, there was talk of the future and decisions about it, often a quite distant future. By adding a time dimension, it becomes easier to create tolerance for the discrepancies among talk, decisions, and actions. Time creates order among what is said, decided, and done—an order we recognize. The traditional concept that talk and decisions increase the likelihood of a certain action implies a time dimension—the time between cause and effect—even if this time is usually thought to be shorter than the five to fifteen years in some of the examples above. This perception of time creates the hope that what is done will one day be consistent with what is said and the decisions that are made—that there will finally be implementation.

The question is, of course, what happens when the future becomes the present? Is it possible to maintain the discrepancy between the decision and the action or will we be forced to finally act in accordance with the decision? Is hypocrisy unstable in the long run as a result of implementation?

Traditional assumptions lead us to expect instability. Talk and decisions should, at least in the long run, lead to consistent actions. Goals are eventually met. Talk and decisions govern our actions, even if it takes time. In the long run, we practice what we preach. If we do not like hypocrisy, or if we think that what the actor says and decides is more appealing than how the actor acts, this is an optimistic assumption. Morally superior talk and decisions can, for example, been seen as a preparatory stage to similarly virtuous actions.[23]

[22] N. Brunsson and Sahlin-Andersson (2000).   [23] March 1978.

Hypocrisy can be unstable in this way. Even in a distant future people may refer to the decisions made long ago and demand that they should be implemented, and this could force belated implementation. Thus the decision is, in the long run, matched by the corresponding action.

In many contexts, however, old decisions are not implemented, and hypocrisy is stable. In a distant future, it is likely that most people will think that the situation has changed too much for the old decisions to be tenable, and that the whole situation must be re-evaluated in its current context. A combination of long-term planning by the decision-makers and faith in rapid change with those making demands contributes to the irrelevancy of the decisions at the time when they should be implemented. Thus the old decisions have no effect on the current demands, and there is a low probability of implementation.

Decisions can also lose their importance by being forgotten, probably not an uncommon scenario. It happens even in parliaments, where decision-making is the very task of the organization, where decisions are recorded carefully, and where different parties exist, some of which have a vested interest in reminding everyone of the decision once made.[24]

If the new situation involves continued conflicting demands, it is not unlikely that any possible reminders of previous decisions will lead to renewed hypocrisy. The response may be a new decision to actually implement a previous decision. Olson[25] showed how a city responded to concurrent demands for a balanced economy and for increased resources to meet urgent needs by deciding on a strict budget, while actually allowing expenditure to increase. When complaints about the economy were filed, new, even more forceful and restrictive decisions were made about the budget. In practice, however, expenditures continued to increase. This pattern was repeated for several years.

One example of long-term memory where the result was continued hypocrisy is the issue of nuclear power in Sweden. In a 1980 referendum, Swedes voted on whether to allow nuclear power in the country. The alternative to increase Swedish nuclear power capacity to the largest per capita in the world turned out to be the winning one. The propaganda for this decision alternative stated that nuclear power would be abolished in twenty-five years. Interpreted according to the hypocrisy model, the prerequisite to gaining support for the expansion was to make the opposite decision: to dismantle. It may seem that twenty-five years is a safe distance, but yet, twenty years later there were people who asserted that the old decision should be respected and that the implementation should now begin. The counterarguments made some impression: that many of those who were once part of the majority were

[24] K. Brunsson (1994, 1998).   [25] Olson (1996).

now deceased, and that no one now under the age of 38 had been allowed to vote. And the issue was no longer as well discussed or as controversial as it had been twenty years earlier. The result was that the state forced the shutdown of one small, privately owned nuclear power plant (about 6% of the total national capacity) and once again decided that all nuclear power plants must be shut down in the future. (However, this time there was no time limit imposed; it was just decided that viable alternative energy sources had to become available first.) At the same time, other old, larger plants were thoroughly renovated in order to secure continued long-time production. On the whole, the old strategy was repeated.

It is also possible to react to reminders of prior decisions by implementing the corresponding action, while at the same time talking and making decisions that are contrary to it. Hypocrisy is still used but with new contents in decisions and actions in a zigzagging type of motion. One set of inconsistencies among talk, decision, and action is simply replaced by another. If the city of Stockholm would have to implement its old decision and actually reduce city traffic, it would help to make a new decision of increased availability to the city by car in fifteen years.

Justification

Implementation destabilizes hypocrisy by actions being adapted to previous talk and decisions. But hypocrisy may also be destabilized by justification: by adapting talk and decisions to the action that has been carried out. Although an action differs from talk and decisions that preceded it, it can be defended and decided upon in hindsight.

Justification may be an effect of positively endogenous preferences: the fact that something has been done makes us like it.[26] Then it is not prior decisions that affect which demands are made on an organization, as discussed above; instead demands are formed by previous action. Action influences demands in a positive direction so that they become concurrent with the implemented action, reducing or abolishing conflict. There is no longer need for hypocrisy. Even if at the outset we have talked and decided differently than we acted, we can now begin to talk and decide as we have just acted. In accordance with traditional decision theory talk, decisions, and actions become consistent, but in contrast to this theory consistency is achieved by talk and decisions being adapted to action instead of the other way round. We are not practising what we preached but we are preaching what we practised. Hypocrisy has facilitated actions that reduce the need for further hypocrisy.

[26] March (1978).

The Norm of Consistency

Another threat to the stability of hypocrisy is the norm of consistency—the norm that actors should not be hypocrites. There is always the risk that hypocrisy will be discovered, thought to be a major sin, and sanctioned. That danger creates a certain incentive for the hypocritical organization finally to adapt its actions to what has been decided or talked about, or vice versa.

However, the attention needed to discover hypocrisy is a scarce resource. As mentioned, it is easy to forget what was once said and what was once decided upon, and it is not always easy for one individual to know about all talk, decisions, and actions of an organization. This is especially true if no one is interested in monitoring organizational behaviour. Sometimes the media function as monitors. It is a classic story for the press to report on inconsistencies and to do so with negative overtones, contributing to the destabilization of hypocrisy.

Once hypocrisy has been discovered, its stability is dependent on the extent to which it is tolerated and sanctioned. If there is a superordinate hierarchical level that can sanction hypocrisy, instability increases. Sometimes a court system with the power to demand that certain decisions (i.e. contracts) produce corresponding action, effectively ends hypocrisy or attempts at hypocrisy. Krasner[27] showed how nation states have long demonstrated hypocrisy by claiming to have strong 'Westphalian sovereignty', which, in practice, they have often acted against. Krasner argued that the lack of a higher level supra-state, the lack of a world state, has contributed to the fact that hypocrisy regarding sovereignty has been ongoing for centuries. No one has had the power to punish the hypocrites. Similarly, Machiavelli[28] argued that the actions of the sovereigns—who were not under any court—were particularly unlikely to be judged by their consistency with the sovereigns' talk.

Without superordinate hierarchical levels, there are varying degrees of intolerance and tolerance; tolerance varies somewhat for various organizations and for various outside parties.

In general, because the norm of consistency is a norm for actors, tolerance of hypocrisy is lower the more the organization is seen across space and time to be an actor. The tolerance of hypocrisy can be assumed to be very weak for a corporate management team that presents itself as unified, supreme, and with the power to micro-manage its subordinates: then the company really seems to be one actor. Hypocrisy in this case seems to be intentional. The tolerance for hypocrisy can be assumed to be higher for a state that is led by a minority government with weak control instruments. Such a state seems more like an

---

[27] Krasner (1999).   [28] Machiavelli (1513: ch. XVIII).

arena for different interests, and it does not seem reasonable to expect that much consistency. Instead, the tolerance for hypocrisy is lower for those who are perceived as the real actors on the arena, politicians or political parties for example.

In a similar fashion, the perception of whether we are dealing with one actor or many over time can influence the tolerance of hypocrisy. If the state had changed its administration, we would be more tolerant of inconsistency because we would not expect the new government to always act in accordance with decisions made by the old one: we tend to think that a new actor has been created, and interpret what has happened as an inconsistency between actors rather than the hypocrisy of one actor.

On the other hand, if tolerance of hypocrisy is high because there are doubts as to whether the organization is really an actor, the organization does not have much use for it. As argued above, it is the presumed actorhood of an organization that makes hypocrisy work for materialists. If they do not believe that it is one and the same actor that talks, makes decisions, and acts, they have little reason to expect consistency and therefore little reason to pay attention to talk and decisions.

Tolerance for hypocrisy also varies among those setting demands for organizations. Most of these people or groups are interested in specific talk, decisions, and actions, not merely in upholding the norm of non-hypocrisy. The general, normative demand that the organization should not be hypocritical is not always strong compared to the more concrete demands about the ways in which the organization handles specific issues: the more concrete demands are often those likely to win out. Those who believe that their concrete demands are being met are less likely to care whether the organization is being hypocritical or not; whereas those who believe that their demands are not being met will accuse the organization of hypocrisy. For instance, those who hope for a certain action are likely to be pleased with this action regardless of whether hypocrisy is involved or not.

Therefore, we can expect that the total tolerance for hypocrisy is lowest when the specific contents of talk, decision, and action are of least interest. At that point, there is no one prepared to accept hypocrisy merely because it happens to favour a concrete issue of their personal interest. The huge scandals, during which many people question the actors' methods and honour, will be those concerned with talk, decisions, and actions that no one really cares about. This mechanism would explain the otherwise surprising fact that a politician who is a hypocrite in private life is often condemned by more people than is a politician who is hypocritical in seemingly more important matters that actually concern outsiders. The unusual demand to impeach former US President Clinton occurred when he lied about his personal relationships, not when he facilitated trade with communist China while talking about the importance of defending human rights in that country. In Swedish politics, the government's nuclear power policy has not led to any ministerial resignations, but Swedish ministers have lost office when they have been accused of not practising what they preached in their private lives: for instance when they have been involved in (legal) tax planning or bought the wrong kind of private apartment. It is safer to be a hypocrite about things that are perceived to be important than to be one about things that are perceived to be unimportant.

EVALUATING HYPOCRISY

The word 'hypocrisy' has a negative ring. It is easy to condemn it quickly as both immoral and problematic. But upon closer inspection, hypocrisy does not appear to reside so clearly on the dark side.

Hypocrisy creates opportunities. It facilitates action in conflict situations. Certain actions would not be possible if contrary talk and decisions were not possible. But hypocrisy also makes talk and decisions possible. It would be impossible to talk or to make decisions about certain things if the contrary action was not simultaneously possible. Hypocrisy offers a high degree of freedom. Instead of talk, decisions, and actions governing each other in one set direction, there are two possible directions. Individuals or organizations are not forced to talk and make decisions that always correspond to actions, and they are not forced to act as they talk and decide. It makes other talk, decisions, and actions possible than if the three should have to be consistent.

Whether this increased freedom is positive or negative is open to debate. I have argued that hypocrisy can be seen not only as a problem but as a solution. It has been argued that it is hypocrisy that sustains established social institutions.[29] And the hypocrisy option improves the likelihood of legitimacy for organizations that work in environments of conflict. Also, if an organization that was subject to contradictory demands, talked, made decisions, and acted in accordance with one of those demands only, the other demands would remain unsatisfied. Those who thought that those demands were legitimate would probably not think that this was a favourable outcome.

Hypocrisy seems to be more problematic when organizations are to be controlled from the outside and from the top down. It is in conflict with the standard formal construction of organizations according to which people at the top of the organizational hierarchy have the right to exercise power and that they do so by making decisions that should then be implemented

---

[29] Shklar (1984).

in action. People choose political organs that have the task of deciding what the government should do. Shareholders choose a general meeting that in turn chooses a board of directors that has as its task to run the company through the decisions it makes. Potential conflicts are to be dealt with in the decision-making process only. In such a structure, hypocrisy clearly seems to be a problem.

Thus, the existence of hypocrisy poses a difficulty for all those who want to influence the actions of an organization via its formal decision-making system, whether they are decision-makers or internal or external lobbyists. If there is no risk of hypocrisy, lobbyists can work through talk and decisions. They can attempt to induce organizations to talk in accordance with the action that they wish to see implemented and they can attempt to convince them to make decisions to that effect, thereby increasing the likelihood of the desired action actually taking place. If, however, there is a risk of hypocrisy, such attempts can become counterproductive. If the lobbyists succeed in convincing the decision-makers to make the right decision, there is a risk that they will lose the chance of seeing the desired action actually carried out. For example, it is uncertain whether those who desire that city traffic be decreased should actually work for a decision to decrease traffic, or if they should frenetically try to counteract such a decision, and perhaps work for the opposite decision. Awareness of the chance or risk of hypocrisy is an important insight both for external lobbying groups and those who want to influence the actions of their own organizations.

The relationship between hypocrisy and morality is an ambiguous one. Hypocrisy can be seen as morally wrong. But a complete lack of hypocrisy has also been defined as fanaticism, as too strong a commitment to one's values.[30] And, just like sin, hypocrisy can even be seen as a prerequisite for sound morals. If we do not allow ourselves to possess and propagate higher values than those portrayed by our actions—if we do not allow for sin and hypocrisy—then we run the risk of not having very high morals at all.[31] Hypocrisy makes it possible to talk and to make decisions about high values, even for those who do not act in accordance with these values. If only the few who act in accordance with high values are allowed to support them, substantially fewer people can express their support. Hypocrisy can be seen as 'a tribute that vice pays to virtue'.[32] Morality does not necessarily gain from the cessation of hypocrisy. If we have previously talked and made decisions that were more moral than our actions, then the cessation of hypocrisy means that we are now talking and making decisions that are as immoral as our actions.

---

[30] Newman (1986).   [31] Matt. (5: 17–48).
[32] L'hypocrisie est un hommage que le vice rend à la vertu (La Rochefoucauld 1665: 218).

For example, hypocrisy makes it possible for a company with a polluting production and product (e.g. a car producer) to establish environmental plans and to decide upon environmental goals. Without hypocrisy, it would admit that its operations were environmentally hazardous, that it planned to continue these operations, and it would have to defend them as being necessary and unavoidable. Then many people would probably think that the company polluted not only the physical environment but the moral environment as well.

Hypocrisy relating to moral issues can be perceived to be better than justification in situations in which we have higher values than we can live by. If we are to have high values, hypocrisy seems to be as unavoidable as is sin. But it is commonly held that we should not *strive for* hypocrisy or sin. That is a maxim by which we can try to live our own lives. But when we are observers of others, it is often difficult to judge what is intended and what is result.

REFERENCES

Arnold, T. W. (1937). *The Folklore of Capitalism*. Westport, CT: Yale University Press.

Austin, J. L. (1962). *How to do Things with Words*. Cambridge, MA: Harvard University press.

Brunsson, K. (1994). Organizational Oblivion. Paper presented to the SCOS conference, Calgary.

——(1998). 'Non-learning Organizations', *Scandinavian Journal of Management*, 14(4): 421–32.

Brunsson, N. (1986). 'Organizing for Inconsistencies. On Organizational Conflict, Depression and Hypocrisy as Substitutes for Action', *Scandinavian Journal of Management Studies*, 2(3/4): 165–85.

——(1995). 'Ideas and Actions: Justification and Hypocrisy as Alternatives to Control', in S. B. Bacharach, P. Gagliardi, and B. Mundell (eds.), *Studies of Organizations: The European Tradition*. Greenwich, CT: JAI Press.

——(2002). *The Organization of Hypocrisy: Talk, Decisions and Actions in Organizations*, 2nd edn. Oslo: Abstrakt, Liber, Copenhagen, Business School Press. First published by Wiley 1989.

—— and Sahlin-Andersson, K. (2000). 'Constructing Organizations: The Example of Public Sector Reform', *Organization Studies*, 21(4): 721–46.

Cyert, R. M. and March, J. G. ([1963] 1992). *A Behavioral Theory of the Firm*. Oxford: Blackwell.

Czarniawska-Joerges, B. (1990). 'Merchants of Meaning: Management Consulting in the Swedish Public Sector', in B. A. Turner (ed.), *Organizational Symbolism*. New York: de Gruyter, pp. 139–50.

Edelman, M. (1964). *The Symbolic Uses of Politics*. Urbana: University of Illinois Press.

Friedlander, F. and Pickle, H. (1968). 'Components of Effectiveness in Small Organizations', *Administrative Science Quarterly*, 13: 289–304.

Garme, C. (2001). *Newcomers to Power. Socialists Conquer France in 1981, non-Socialists Conquer Sweden in 1976*. Uppsala, Sweden: Acta Universitas Uppsaliensis.

Holmblad Brunsson, K. (2002). 'Management or Politics or Both? How Management by Objectives May be Managed: A Swedish Example', *Financial Accountability & Management*, 18(2): 189–209.

Krasner, S. (1999). *Sovereignty. Organized Hypocrisy*. Princeton, NJ: Princeton University Press.

La Rochefoucauld, F. (1665). *Maximes*.

Loewenstein, G. and Elster, J. (eds.) (1992). *Choice Over Time*. New York: Sage.

Machiavelli, N. (1513). *Il Principe*. (English translation by George Bull: *The Prince*. London: Penguin Classics, 1999).

March, J. G. (1978). 'Bounded Rationality, and Ambiguity and the Engineering of Choice', *Bell Journal of Economics*, 9: 587–608.

Matthew. The Gospel according to St Matthew. 5: 17–48.

Meyer, J. (1996). 'Otherhood: The Promulgation and Transmission of Ideas in the Modern Organizational Environment', in B. Czarniawska and G. Sevón (eds.), *Translating Organizational Change*. Berlin: de Gruyter.

_____ Boli, J. and Thomas, G. M. (1987). 'Ontology and Rationalization in the Western Account', in G. M. Thomas, J. W. Meyer, Francisco O. Ramírez, and J. Boli (eds.), *Institutional Structure: Constituting State, Society, and the Individual*. Newbury Parks, CA: Sage.

_____ and Rowan, B. (1977). 'Institutionalized Organizations: Formal Structure as Myth and Ceremony', *American Journal of Sociology*, 83(2): 340–63.

Newman, J. (1986). *Fanatics & Hypocrites*. Buffalo, NY: Prometheus Books.

Olson, O. (1996). 'Forandring i Bergen kommune', in O. Olson and F. Mellemvik (eds.), *Regnskap i forandring. Utveckling spredning och bruk av kommuneregnskap*. Oslo: Cappelen Akademisk forlag.

Rombach, B. (1991). *Det går inte att styra med mål!*, Lund, Sweden: Studentlitteratur.

Sartori, G. (1962). *Democratic Theory*. Westport, CT: Greenwood Press.

Shklar, J. N. (1984). *Ordinary Vices*. Cambridge, MA: Harvard University Press.

Strang, D. and Meyer, J. (1993). 'Institutional Conditions for Diffusion', *Theory and Society*, 22: 487–511.

The Concise Oxford Dictionary of Current English ([1976] 1995). Oxford: Clarendon Press.

Veyne, P. (1983). *Les Grecs ont-ils cru à leurs mythes? Essai sur l'imagination constituante*. Paris: Editions de Seuil.

Weick, K. E. (1976). 'Educational Organizations as Loosely Coupled Systems', *Administrative Science Quarterly*, 21: 1–19.

Whitehouse News Release 20020305–6.

Wildavsky, A. (1975). *Budgeting. A comparative Theory of Budgetary Processes*. Boston, MA: Little, Brown and Company.

8

Ideas and Actions: Justification and Hypocrisy as Alternatives to Control

An important idea running through much Western thought attributes a body–soul dichotomy to the human make-up: the soul is the locus of thought and ideas, the body the instrument of action. Human beings produce, reproduce, and cherish ideas about the world—what it is like and what it should be like. They act routinely or heroically, alone or together with others. Ideas and actions are envisaged as separate and essentially different phenomena, but are also seen as related in normative or descriptive terms. Ideas may reflect actions; they may report on them and provide them with meaning. Actions may reflect ideas; they can materialize wishes or predictions.

It is generally assumed that human beings are 'individuals': they hold a number of relatively stable and specific preferences which, together with their notions of what the situation is like, will guide their actions. People apply their ideas in choosing their actions. Consistency obtains between their ideas and their actions, and it is the ideas that control the actions. These conditions are an essential part, albeit not the whole, of what is labelled rationality.

This individual conception of the way ideas and actions are related to one another is also often used in describing or prescribing the behaviour of groups of people, such as organizations or societies, often referred to as 'legal persons'. Organizations and societies are understood in a similar way as are single human beings. If the people constituting the group are also envisaged as individuals, they will be expected to have different preferences and other conceptions. Coordinated group action then requires communication, that is, that the ideas that are to be turned into action are expressed and heard.

When the soul and body model is used for constructing organizations and societies, it leads to a division of labour between thinkers and doers. It is one task to provide ideas; it is another to act. Often certain people are authorized to carry out the first task and others the second. The first group forms a constituency which is supposed to articulate ideas to be realized by the second group, the actors. The constituency can have different forms and names: it could consist of owners of a joint-stock company, of members of an association or of voters in a democracy. Often two other parties are involved:

representatives of the constituency form a board of directors, a general assembly or a parliament; and sometimes there is an executive of managers or politicians who are supposed to link the ideas of the constituency and its representatives into the actions of the actors. The constituency–representative–executive–actor structure is supposed to form a chain of successive principals and agents.

This constituency–actor structure reflects the concept of the rational individual, but the need for communication means that the tasks are a little different from those of the single human being. Ideas not only have to be thought up by the constituency and its representatives; they also need to be talked about. The representatives and executives cannot content themselves with making choices; they also have to put them into words, to declare them as decisions. These last are then a signal for action to the actors, but they may also be a way of describing, of accounting for, the choices before the constituency. And the constituency, the representatives and the executive can all be expected to be interested in what actions are actually carried out, which means that these too must be described.

The constituency–actor structure is a standard one in organizations and in politics. It constitutes an important argument in legitimizing coordination: coordination involves a certain degree of subordination on the part of people who believe in their own individuality and want to emphasize it; recognizing the free individual as part of the constituency compensates for the lack of individuality in the actor functions. And since individual human beings play both roles, and since their ideas are assumed to influence decisions about what actions are to be taken, they can be regarded to some extent as controlling their own actions. In this way the apparently powerful conflict between human beings as individuals on the one hand and organizations and societies as individuals on the other can be substantially reduced. The argument builds on the individual-rational assumptions regarding the relationship between ideas and actions: that the constituency's ideas and the actors' actions are consistent with each other, and that this consistency is achieved because the constituency ideas control the actions, and not the other way round.

Much thought and activity has been devoted to the more intricate problems of these assumptions. For example, is it at all practically possible to differentiate so clearly between ideas and actions (Harmon 1989)? How can an open discussion within the constituency and its representatives be organized so that different ideas can be expressed, and how can we determine which ideas among a number of different and contradictory ones should be consistent with action and in a position to control it? How can the representatives' ideas become representative of those of the constituency? The purpose of this chapter is not to answer all these questions—it is considerably less ambitious.

I indicate a few problems that can arise once we know what the relevant ideas are. And the discussion will remain on a fairly simple level compared to all the complexities which we could envisage or could meet in practice. Most noticeably, perhaps, the possibility of conflicts among representatives, executives, or actors will be largely disregarded.

It is not easy either for individuals or for groups structured as described above to reconcile ideas and actions. The world of ideas is very different from the world of action. Three differences in particular between the conditions for ideas and action can create difficulties in achieving consistency and control. The first concerns the actual content of ideas and actions. What can be talked about cannot always be translated into action, and what can be done cannot always be talked about, a difference that affects the possibility of achieving consistency. Second, ideas may develop one way in contexts in which ideas are of central importance, and in another way in contexts in which action is the more crucial. This can give rise to problems of control. Finally, ideas may sometimes arise and change and disappear more rapidly than actions. This affects the possibility of reconciling consistency with control. As possible and partial solutions to these problems I refer to two other relations between ideas and actions besides consistency and control, namely justification and hypocrisy. The discussion will focus on the problem as it affects groups with a constituency–actor structure although some problems may be similar to those experienced by individual human beings.

THE PROBLEM OF CONSISTENCY: WHAT CAN BE SAID BUT NOT DONE AND WHAT CAN BE DONE BUT NOT SAID

A fundamental although little discussed or problematized assumption in models of rationality is that it is possible to formulate ideas, such as preferences or notions of consequences. In the model of constituency and actors, this assumption turns into a requirement regarding openness or frankness: ideas must be expressed before they can be transformed into action. It is also often felt to be important that open discussion should take place, a free debate in which different opinions are put forward and scrutinized, and that the view adopted according to the majority principle or accepted as a fair compromise is then realized in action. A basic condition of this model is that it is possible to say the same things as it is possible to do. This condition is not always met.

It is perhaps easiest to recognize that much which can be said cannot be done. Many discussions of ideas which take place at a distance from action, are full of opinions expressing desires and norms rather than facts and forecasts. Indeed, this is an important function of many debates, for instance among political representatives: they are meant as an expression of different values and ideas in the constituency, not simply as an attempt to determine what has happened or is going to happen (Olsen 1991: ch. 1). And for many reasons a lot of these wishes may be impossible to convert into action.

One reason could be lack of knowledge. Even if we have a certain understanding of what ought to be done or how the world ought to be, it is not certain that we know how to bring this about. For instance, political debate is typically full of such ambitions; it often involves a desire to solve major social problems—anything from drug abuse to the avoidance of economic recession—which no one has so far been able to solve. The difficulty of solving certain problems often makes these more rather than less important to discuss.

Action often demands more resources, time, and power than ideas; ideas are cheaper than actions. Wishes can be presented but not implemented because of a shortage of resources such as money or people. Or time may be lacking; ideas can be quickly stated, but action can sometimes take so long that problems fail to be solved in time, and opportunities are missed. And even if both resources and time are available, there may still be a lack of the power necessary to influence those who can act.

In many social settings, what is said is more contradictory than what is done. A discussion may contain many differing and contradictory views and interpretations. The opinions of the important people or the majority may also change quickly over time. It may be more difficult to act in a contradictory way. Contradictory actions are the opposite of what we usually call efficiency; they consume more resources than contradictory talk and so are often more difficult to bring about.

Thus, broadly speaking, some of the main reasons for things being said but not done are economic; they are associated with limitations in knowledge, resources, and opportunities for control. A limited supply of these factors makes it difficult to move on from idea to action. By creating a specific arena for discussion which is disengaged from action, we encourage ideas of little feasibility; room is provided for plenty of wishes, ambitions, visions, and contradictory ideas, all of which are difficult to convert into action.

Furthermore, there is little evidence that feasible ideas are particularly likely to gain the widest support. On the contrary, many debates are won by those who have the best ideas, not by those who adapt their ideas to what is feasible. The best ideas are those which most successfully express the good, the just, and the beautiful rather than the realistic, pragmatic, and feasible; the best ideas are often most difficult to convert into action. Views which are adapted to what is popular in the current situation, without making any allowance for the fact that they conflict with other opinions popular in other situations, have greater chances of winning support than opinions which are inflexible over time and in a variety of situations and fashions. It may also be easier to gain wide support for ideas which are vague and simple, but such ideas do not offer much direction for action (Baier, March, and Saetren 1986). Or it may be easy to make a compromise between various contradictory opinions in order to win over the majority, but such compromises may well be more difficult to carry over into action: one cannot, for example, both do and fail to do something.

What Can Be Done But Not Said

The fact that things can be done but not said is connected with ethics, aesthetics, and truth. Ethical norms tend to limit what we can say, more than what we can do. It is easier to implement actions which are regarded as immoral, than to acknowledge them openly; and it is even more difficult to defend them or to propose that they be adopted. In other words, it is difficult to hold an open discussion about actions which are difficult to defend on morally acceptable grounds. This difficulty can lead to things being done without their being openly accounted for.

On the other hand, this does not necessarily contradict the idea of consistency between the opinions of the constituency and the actions taken; people may want immoral acts to occur. For instance, shareholders may want the company to use bribes in order to secure important business even if they are not likely to argue for such a practice. Or, if in national politics it is considered impossible to provide a moral defence of arms exports to certain countries, then the export must happen in secret. Such secrecy runs counter to ideas about open debate, but need not lead to inconsistency between ideas and actions; it may be that a large majority believe that the advantages of arms export outweigh its dubious morality.

So the fact that we cannot say certain things does not mean that we cannot do them or believe that they ought to be done. But the absence of open discussion makes it difficult to see how far opinions and actions really correspond. And when actions are secret, people other than the actors are prevented from discovering any possible discrepancy between what they think and what is being done.

Sometimes, too, things can be done in a completely open way but still cannot be defended. This also hampers open discussion. Opponents who invoke moral arguments against an operation are not met by any moral counterarguments, and they therefore risk feeling disregarded or not being taken seriously. Those who try to use moral arguments in a debate on transport policy are hardly met with ethical counterarguments: arguments emphasizing the major losses in terms of people's lives and injuries in road transport, often meet with arguments of accessibility, time savings and costs, and silence as to how this is to be measured against human suffering.

In other cases, what we say may influence action even if we do not wish so. If executives have to talk according to ethical standards, this may make actors act accordingly, even if these actions do not reflect what the executives really want. In these cases a consistency between talk and action produces an inconsistency between executive opinion and action.

There are also actions which are not usually discussed for what could be called aesthetic reasons. These obviously vary in different cultures, at different times and in different social situations. Organizations often contain norms regulating what can be discussed; some actions are undiscussable even if they are not directly unethical. Sometimes generalization is such a norm for some representatives or executives: only broad principles are to be discussed, not individual actions or specific details. Some groups are supposed to discuss future actions rather than past ones. Employees do not talk about sensible actions they undertake which do not fit into the image of the organization. Or subordinates do not tell bosses that they do not follow their unwise orders.

Some of the actions which are not discussed for aesthetic reasons may be regarded as 'human' or 'natural' and therefore acceptable as actions, but it still does not make them presentable. Such aesthetic norms can have the same effect as moral norms on the opportunities for open discussion and the possibility of creating consistency between ideas and actions.

Truth and Practice

Much talk and many discussions are also limited by the demand for truth: what can be said must be true. A requirement of this nature might at first appear to imply that what can be said can also be done. But what is regarded as true is not always determined by what happens in practice. The truth, at least the official truth, which can be referred to in public statements or debates, may sometimes deviate to a considerable degree from what could be called the private truth, which is based on people's own experience. What is considered to be true is often determined by well-established and shared assumptions in a society; the official truth is part of what are known as social institutions. Institutions are sometimes described as consistent units—sets of ideas about how the world is constructed which generate rules about how to act and thus also a corresponding pattern of action, which in turn strengthens the ideas and the rules (Berger and Luckmann 1966: ch. II, p. 1). But such consistency is not always obtained. Instead, patterns of action may be obviously at odds with ideas, or at least with ideas and opinions which are presentable in public. If discussion is to meet the requirement of keeping to the official institution-alized truth, the result may be a situation in which what can be done cannot be said.

It is not difficult to find examples of institutionally determined official truths which can deviate considerably from everyday practice. A common-place example, referred to in the introduction, is the institutionalized con-ception in our culture of people as fairly rational individuals possessing reasonably stable and unique personal characteristics and values. This means that people have to present themselves and their actions in a manner that corresponds to this kind of model (Meyer, Boli, and Thomas 1987). They are expected to be able to present reasonably stable values as well as inten-tions. They should be able to present their actions as the result of conscious choices based on specific goals and intentions—they are expected to be able to 'rationalize' their actions. But it can hardly be claimed that a model of this type provides a very good description of human behaviour in practice (Cyert and March 1963; Nisbett and Ross 1980). Rationality would in fact make development impossible, for example, from the child to the adult individual (March 1978); it would also make action more difficult (Brunsson 1985).

As described in the introduction, formal organizations such as companies and public agencies are also usually presented as rational individuals—as coherent entities, easily distinguishable from their environment, controlled from above by their leaders and their ideas, goal-oriented and basing their actions on rational decisions. At any rate it would be difficult for the leaders of organizations to deny that they ought to strive to make their organizations work in this way. But, as organizational research has told us in the last few decades, none of this prevents organization members from behaving in a com-pletely different way in practice, for instance by reflecting their institutional environments (Meyer and Rowan 1977), building strong informal networks across organizational boundaries (Håkansson 1989), avoiding control from above (Selznick [1949] 1965) or making decisions in a systematically irrational way (Brunsson 1985). Such behaviour may be necessary and extremely useful in many situations, but it cannot be adopted when organizations are being presented to the outside world.

The market is another institution in which there can be a considerable difference between presentation and practice. Certain patterns of action in connection with purchasing and selling were long considered morally dubious and could therefore be adopted but not defended (Segal 1990). They involved such things as striving for personal gain, disloyalty, and short-term actions. Mandeville (1724) attempted to show that such patterns of action in just the market context were in fact respectable, in that they led to good results. Such ideas are now commonplace; formerly dubious patterns of action are now described as worth striving for and as characteristic of actual behaviour on markets. They can be both said and done.

Now, instead, there are other behaviours which can be adopted but not declared but this time because they are untrue rather than or as well as being immoral. Modern markets exhibit obvious signs of loyalty, long-term relations, and control between sellers and buyers (Hägg and Johanson 1982; Håkansson 1989). Such behaviour may perhaps be discussed in terms of problems, but it is not part of the official truth about markets, of the way markets can be discussed and displayed. This truth contains a strong element of disloyalty, short-term relations and disconnectedness between sellers and buyers (Granovetter 1985). Even if people have devoted all their working lives to long-term cooperation and control over their customers and suppliers, they are not very likely to be able to use this experience in any open discussion of markets in general.

The truth about markets is determined to a high degree by scientific theories, produced in a tradition of ideal types and model rigour, and this adds to the difference between truth and practice. The difference between truth and practice can generally be expected to increase when institutions are described scientifically, and when these scientific descriptions are extended to professions, opinion leaders, and leaders. Scientific theories are seldom much use to practical action. They provide explanations rather than understanding, and only understanding can give a basis for action (Sandelands 1990). In addition, scientific theories normally describe aspects of reality, not the totalities needed for sensible action. But the one-dimensional nature of theories does facilitate clarity, simplicity, and logic, and these qualities backed up by the great authority of science can lead to the theories becoming attractive as opinions and easily understood as truths. A variety of theories, some more extreme than others on complicated subjects such as formal organizations (Scott 1992) or how to bring up children (Hirdman 1989) have succeeded each other throughout the twentieth century, and although they have presumably had some effect on organizational and parental practices, we can assume (and hope) that these practices have been more complex and stable as well as better suited to the overall conditions and practical needs of individual organizations and children than any one of the theories has been. This suggests that large areas of practice have never been publicly displayed. In the light of scientific descriptions, personal experience—however relevant to actual practice—easily comes to seem irrelevant to 'serious' discourse, or it is thought to represent uninteresting exceptions which do not influence the principles and general rules under discussion.

The fact that practical experience does not acquire a truth value high enough for public display can have different effects in different contexts. One may be that discussion and action remain separate; to those who act discussion seems as irrelevant as practice does to those who talk. Another may be that certain ideas which are based on practical experience and practical frames of reference cannot be expressed or understood in discussions. In discussions about the future of savings banks, for example, operations were defined by leading actors in terms of the company institution, in which competition, customers, growth, and profitability are all important factors. Others based their conception of savings banks on older ideas and on long experience of working in such banks. They saw savings banks as concerned more with social welfare than with business. Although these people had opposing views on concrete actions, they could seldom express them; they could put up passive resistance but could not make any kind of serious protest—their preferred actions could not be defended (Forssell 1989).

Reforms—officially proclaimed attempts to change practice—must follow the norms for what can be said. If they are directed at areas where the differences between what can be said and what can be done are big, they risk being irrelevant to practice and therefore impossible to implement. The people whose practices are to be reformed do not see the point of the reform and may offer passive resistance; they do not allow themselves to be provoked into either discussion or change. In such situations real change can only be brought about quietly without any proclamation of reform. Although the reform ideas do not lead to any practical effects, they can be spread easily and widely (good ideas are easy to talk about), thus reinforcing the impression that they are true. Information about real change in practices is more difficult to spread around and therefore difficult to learn from.

But sometimes talk may influence action, making the two consistent. For example, established practice is not always powerful enough to render reforms ineffective. Reforms can influence practice if the practitioners are forced to take part in the related discussions. If earlier practices cannot be defended, there is a risk that they will disappear. The reforms can result in a situation in which what is done assumes a closer resemblance to what can be said. This was the result in the case of the savings banks.

But just as in the case of ethical and aesthetical norms, consistency between talk and action does not guarantee consistency between ideas and actions. People may not hold beliefs and wishes that are in accordance with what is officially true, even if they have to talk that way. In these cases, consistency between talk and action produces inconsistency between their opinions and action.

For example, reforms can lead to new practices even if a majority (or in principle everyone) is against such changes. Not even the reformers themselves need to hold the opinions which are launched in the reforms. Professional reformers who proposed reforms aimed at raising the level of rationality in organizations, themselves behaved with systematic irrationality when they were selling and implementing their reforms (Brunsson and Olsen 1993: chs. 5–6). Moreover, they had well-developed private theories, never officially displayed, about why irrational practices were the best. This did not stop them from arguing very powerfully for rational reforms. After all, reforms better suited to their real personal appreciation of irrationality would probably have been hard to sell.

As argued above, decisions are a standard executive instrument for transforming ideas into actions. But decisions are complicated to use when there is a difference between what can be said and done. Like any other statements, decisions can only contain what can be said; ideas which cannot be expressed cannot provide the stuff of decisions either. This means that some ideas can never be incorporated into a decision, even if they represent the opinion of a majority of the decision-makers. Thus decisions may sometimes have a content that does not reflect anyone's opinions, just like the reform proposals discussed above. In such cases the implementation of a decision leads to even greater inconsistency between idea and action. The failure of such decisions to control actions becomes a necessary although not a sufficient condition of consistency between ideas and action. In the next section I describe further difficulties in using decisions for transforming ideas into actions.

IDEAS AND ACTION—THE PROBLEM OF CONTROL

The differences between the conditions for talk and action described in the preceeding section highlight the usefulness of the social structure we are examining here: it seems sensible to distinguish between talk and action, perhaps by discussing things on certain occasions and taking action on others, or by letting certain people or organizations or parts of organizations specialize in talk while others specialize in action. But this very distinction creates problems of control—how are we to guarantee that the right ideas do really control action? Modern democracies and public or private large organizations are all characterized by a very sharp distinction between those whose role is to present ideas and those who are to take action. As states and corporations have grown in size, huge administrative apparatuses have emerged whose alleged role is to implement the actions desired by constituencies, representatives, and executives.

So how should discussion, which is often characterized by conflict, unrealistic demands, problems, and vague wishes, control action which requires greater consistency, realism, solutions, and precision? A mechanism which helps to solve this problem is decision-making, at least in principle. Decisions can perhaps reduce variation, inconsistency, and vagueness and express a clear opinion, thus converting debate to the requirements of action. In this way decisions can separate discussion from action, thus facilitating both. Discussion is less disturbed by the requirements of action, and action is less disturbed by discussion. Representatives and executives have a role between ideas and actions and are typically those supposed to make the decisions.

But to achieve the benefits of decisions in practice may be difficult. Decisions often represent a compromise between different views, in which disagreement, vagueness, wishful thinking, and problems all remain, to an extent that makes it extremely difficult to use the decision to control action (Baier, March, and Saetren 1986). And even if a decision is clear-cut, it is still not certain that it can isolate discussion from action. Those who are to take action may well listen to the discussion, and are then quite likely to be influenced by it. They may be convinced by the positive aspects of certain proposals on which no decision is subsequently reached; they can also be influenced by criticism of decisions made, perhaps becoming uncertain about the strength of the present or possible future support that a narrowly accepted decision will enjoy.

All this may reduce the prospects of the decision actually being implemented. But such effects can be reduced or avoided if just one idea is expressed without discussion, or if the discussion is characterized by unanimity, consistency, and an irrational concentration on a single action alternative and its positive consequences (Brunsson 1985). This is difficult to achieve among people embracing a variety of ideas and a certain level of conflict, however, and it may even be actively counteracted in the name of intellectuality or democracy and calls for a free and open debate.

The risk that actors will be influenced by pre-decision discussion more than by the decision itself will be even greater if the actors differ from most of the decision-makers in their view of what should be done. This is no improbable situation. The difference in the demands imposed on ideas by discussion and by action can actually affect the content of the ideas. As we noted in the previous section, people who are free to express ideas without having to take action can often afford to defend views that are more moral, beautiful or true, and less feasible, than the views that the actors have to be guided by. Actors generally have to be experts in their specific field of action—something that is not always required or even expected of the constituency, the representatives or the executive. The views of experts and laymen tend to differ according to their different levels and types of knowledge—of the relevant field and of other fields—as well as to their way of reasoning (March and Olsen 1989: 30). Experts may also have special interests to defend which are different from those of laymen.

All these differences between talk and action, and talkers and actors, may make it very difficult for the former to control the latter. There is a great deal of literature describing the 'problem of implementation', that is, the difficulties faced by decision-makers in getting actors to implement their decisions, either because the actors find it difficult to understand a decision or are unwilling to put it into effect (Pressman and Wildavsky 1973; Hanf and Scharpf 1978). But if decision-makers have reached a stage where they express views different from those of the actors and make decisions in accordance with these views, then a big step towards control has already been taken.

A more difficult problem of control arises if the actors control the opinions of the decision-making executives, or even the representatives or the constituency, thus also controlling the content of decisions. This is not a particularly unlikely contingency, as we have seen: it is sensible for people who want to see their opinions become effective to adapt their ideas to the consistency, the precision, the solutions, and the realism that action requires. Such adaptation calls for knowledge of what can be done. And very often the best if not the only experts are precisely those people or organizations who are to be controlled, namely the actors. If it really has to be ensured that decisions are made which have a chance to control actions, then a dialogue must be established with the actors. This type of dialogue is the rule in most organizations. Administrative units of various kinds prepare issues on which management makes decisions—decisions that same administration then puts into effect. In such a dialogue it may be the actors who control the decision-makers instead of the other way round (Brunsson and Jönsson 1979). This is a typical risk in budget decisions; budgeting easily becomes a means for actors to secure ample resources for actions they want, rather than an instrument for managers to control actors, actions, and spending (Wildavsky 1974; Brunsson 1989: ch. 5). The content of the decision is then whatever suits the actors, rather than the ideas which the decision-makers had when the dialogue began. It is a case of consistency between ideas and actions without the control envisaged in our model—ideas are being controlled by actions rather than the other way round.

Such a situation arises easily when the decision-makers and the actors possess different amounts of the relevant practical knowledge. Experiments have shown that people concerned with transmitting information build up a more complex cognitive structure of what is to be sent than those concerned with receiving it (Zajonc 1960). But people with less knowledge find it difficult to build up a cognitive structure that is more complex than the structure of those with more knowledge. This makes it difficult for executives to function as transmitters while the actors more easily transmit their information to the executives. The executives find it easy to receive information, because it makes their original, relatively simple cognitive structure more complex without their having to reject it. Once in possession of the same information as the actors, it is easy to arrive at the same conclusions about what actions are possible and desirable.

This type of control problem is particularly serious because it is difficult for those who are supposed to be in control to see that it is a problem at all. Because the executives have come to share the views of the actors, they simply see the actors acting in accordance with the views they have come to regard as their own. Instead of appearing problematic, the situation seems to be one of total executive control over the actors. There is thus no incentive to increase control. Instead, problems often arise in the relations between the executives and the representatives, since the representatives have not normally come into such close contact with the actors so as to adopt their ideas. Or, if they have, instead the constituency—the owners, union members, electorate, etc.—may recognize that they lack control over their representatives. Both the constituency and the representatives may find it difficult to establish control over the next party, because once the representatives or the executives have accepted the actors' more complex views, it is difficult to persuade them of any other. And if the representatives engage in detailed discussion with the executives, or the constituency members do so with the representatives, they may find themselves facing exactly the same problem of control as the executives had in their relations with the actors.

COMBINING CONSISTENCY AND CONTROL—THE PROBLEM OF TIME

Ideas and actions can differ in more ways than those considered so far. They can appear, and can change, at different speeds. Ideas may arise and also disappear more quickly than the corresponding actions. As we will see, this causes problems in combining consistency and control. But let us first look at some of the reasons why ideas and actions can develop at different rates.

Ideas and Attention

The individual is envisaged as having certain ideas, and it is usually also assumed that these ideas amount to a fairly coherent unit in logical terms.

But a more realistic picture would often be that certain ideas appear under certain external conditions, and that most of a person's ideas do not therefore tend to be especially stable or consistent. In a rapidly changing world, sensible people's ideas of what should be done can be expected to be flexible. But people's ideas change for other reasons too. It is impossible for people in general or for opinion-moulders, such as the media, to draw attention to all issues simultaneously. At any given moment attention is focused on certain conditions: at other times, other conditions receive attention (Kingdon 1984). Shifting attention leads to shifting opinions. A person may display different opinions at different times, or the views of certain persons or groups become more noticeable than others. Public opinion changes. What ideas are popular in a group or society at a given time can be the result of the interplay of attention to certain problems, solutions, and people (Cohen, March, and Olsen 1972; March and Olsen 1976).

Particular solutions attract more attention at certain times than at others. The problems with which these solutions are associated may remain the same, but the attention paid to certain solutions can lead to just those problems becoming the focus of attention which can best be solved with the help of the 'popular' solutions. Thus in a circular process the popular solutions appear to solve present problems. For instance, in recent years it has been popular to propose deregulation and a 'market' approach as solutions to a string of problems which twenty years or so ago were thought to call for more regulation and political interventions. But when market solutions command the most attention, then problems such as price levels and efficiency also come into focus, rather than questions of justice or equality.

Ideas about solutions can also shift over time when different problems command more attention at different times and each problem is accompanied by specific ideas regarding solutions. When another problem is discussed later, the result may be the proposal and acceptance of new solutions which contradict old ones. Similarly, different problems can activate different groups of talkers who propose their own favourite solutions. Certain problems are handled by particular groups or organizations which possess a specific expertise and represent specific interests, which make them argue for one kind of solutions. When attention is shifted to other problems and other groups and organizations, other solutions become well supported by arguments and therefore attractive.

Action—Implementation and Routinization

Actions differ from ideas in that they are usually described not as something 'existing' but as something recreated each time the particular action occurs.

And yet actions can be more stable and can acquire a shape of longer duration than many ideas. This is particularly common in the case of organizational actions—actions which require organized coordination between a great many people. Actions can take time to come into effect—not only must each person's task be specified, but those who act must be motivated and expectations must be created that the actions will be carried out (Brunsson 1985). It also takes a long time to carry out many actions, and even more time may have to pass before they yield any results.

Organizations usually involve a great many routine actions, often implemented according to written or unwritten rules and therefore requiring little active mobilization. At the same time, though, it can be difficult and time-consuming to change routines. Some routines are connected to the routines of other organizations and require joint effort by several organizations to be changed. Other routines are part of wider societal institutions that change only slowly. When institutions differ in presentation and practice—in what is said and done—change rates in these can also be different, and sometimes this means that ideas are changing quicker than practice.

Control or Consistency

Thus, ideas often change more quickly than it would ever be possible to change actions. Such situations create a conflict between the possibility of ideas controlling actions and the possibility of creating consistency between ideas and actions. If the ideas of the constituency and its representatives and executive are to control actions, they must forego actions. If the ideas change during the time it takes to initiate and implement the actions, then at the time when the actions are being realized, ideas and actions will not be consistent. Practice will be inconsistent with ideas, both at the time when action begins and at the time of its completion. If short-lived ideas initiate slow actions, there is constant discontent: discrepancy between ideas and actions is the reason for action as well as being its result; discontent is a strong incentive for attempts at control, but the result of control is also discontent. If instead simultaneous consistency between ideas and actions is to be achieved, then ideas cannot be allowed to control actions.

In a constituency–actor structure consistency cannot be reached if the actors follow the constituency's opinion when the action commences, since it will not be the same as when the action ends. Avoiding control is thus a necessary, although not a sufficient, condition for consistency between ideas and actions in the future. Those who express ideas, both in constituencies and among representatives and executives, sometimes complain about the difficulty of persuading the actors to act accordingly. But in the situations described here, constituencies, representatives, and executives have to choose between loyal actors with whose actions they are dissatisfied, and disobedient actors with whose actions they are a little more likely to become satisfied.

From the actors' point of view disobedience seems sensible if they know that they are evaluated in retrospect for what they have done rather than for poor obedience at the planning stage. In addition, quickly changing ideas within the constituency or among representatives or executives can easily create an impression among actors that it is impossible, and therefore unnecessary to try, to adapt actions to the demands of these people. Disobedience becomes definitely attractive if the actors regard themselves as able to predict the future ideas of their principals. Disobedience and actions based on correct predictions will make principals satisfied at the end. Or actors may choose to obey ideas that can be implemented quickly, and to be more reluctant to obey ideas that take time to implement.

The problem of time, too, could in principle be solved with the help of decisions. Decisions can be seen as a way of freezing ideas. By making decisions, the executives commit themselves to certain ideas, and this commitment is often supposed to last at least for the time it takes to implement the decision. But such decisions tend to create other problems. They may create or reinforce organizational inflexibility in action. And they make decisions-makers appear as particularly slow thinkers, because decisions cannot prevent other people's views from changing. In other words, consistency between the executives' opinions and actions taken may lead to a lack of consistency between the views expressed by the executives and those held by their constituencies and representatives or by other people observing their behaviour. Executives can then easily give the impression of being conservative, stubborn, or a little lacking in intelligence. The same applies for representatives making decisions under the same conditions.

The belief in the possibility of simultaneous control and consistency seems to be based on the assumption that action can be implemented in less time than it takes ideas to change, whereas in fact the opposite is often true. One way of solving this problem is to adapt reality to the assumption. Decisions can be seen as a means of adaptation, since they can be regarded as an attempt to reduce the speed of change in the relevant ideas. Another solution could be to take action only in areas where ideas are expected to remain fairly stable. Another way could of course be to try to speed up the actions. We might search for organizational designs that make actions less time consuming. We might also choose to take only such actions as can be implemented so quickly that ideas do not have time to change. In many organizations, this would generally apply to the purchase of standard equipment for instance, but less often to large construction projects.

Ambiguity can help conceal the problem. If decisions are ambiguous it is easier to interpret them as consistent with ideas, both when the decision is made and when the action is completed. The same applies if the action is ambiguous, or if its results are. Ambiguous results can perhaps be reported differently on different occasions. Ambiguity implies a reduction in control while the appearance of some consistency may still remain.

A further complication is that the relation between ideas and actions is not normally unidirectional. Ideas may influence action, but action may also influence ideas (March 1978). In fact, action may be an important producer of ideas, more important than a great deal of talk. In any case there may be a great many people or groups who do not react until an action hits them.

Actions can give rise to both consistent and conflicting ideas, to both 'rationalization' and protest. Complete rationalization solves the problem of combining control and consistency; protests make the problem more difficult. But unfortunately the reaction is all too likely to be one of protest. Those who react with opposition have a stronger reason to show their reaction than those who react with agreement. Only the first of these groups have a control problem, since they want to stop the action or to launch a different one. This may mean that protests are more common than applause, which in turn easily gives the impression that people in general, and constituencies in particular, are persistently conservative, sluggish, and opposed to anything new. This impression may be highly misleading, as sometimes revealed when executives or actors try to adapt to the protesters by refraining from the action, and then meet protests from another group.

SOLUTIONS—JUSTIFICATION AND HYPOCRISY

I have now pointed out three problems connected with the relation between ideas and action in the constituency–actor model: the problem of consistency, the problem of control, and the problem of combining consistency and control. The problems are due to differences in what can be said and what can be done; to differences in the conditions for idea-producing and action-producing systems; and to differences in the speed at which ideas and actions are produced.

The problems have no simple solutions, but there are different ways of handling them. Below I will indicate two phenomena that can provide at least partial solutions. These are justification and hypocrisy. Justification solves part of the consistency problem, and hypocrisy solves part of the control problem.

Justification

Justification means that planned or accomplished actions are defended in order to convince people that they are the right ones. Successful justification adapts people's ideas to actions. Actors may justify their actions to executives, executives may justify to representatives, and so forth.

Justification involves two deviations from the simplest model of the relation between constituency and actors. First, the assumption that actors and executives restrict themselves to actions and decisions is abandoned; actors and executives produce and present ideas of their own. Second, the assumption of the unidirectional relation between ideas and action is abandoned; in practice strong influence may proceed not only from ideas to action but also from action to ideas. Successful justification means that the problem of consistency and control is solved by achieving consistency at the expense of control. There is an element of control, but actions are now controlling ideas instead of the other way round.

If actors are experts in their field, there is a strong incentive for them to try to convince others of the advantages of the actions they want to take or have already taken. They will often consider themselves to be right, believing that their expert opinions based on profound insights are superior and more firmly based on the facts than the irrelevant and oversimplified ideas and whims produced by other people. If the justification strategy succeeds, it will also facilitate action and save the actors from criticism.

The justification strategy is attractive to executives and representatives for similar reasons. These may be convinced more easily by the more complicated arguments of the actors than they are by their constituency. It may not even be possible to listen to the constituency: the assumption that the constituency possesses ready-made ideas may not be a realistic one; there may not be any pool of opinions and preferences to draw on. Opinions and preferences may arise only after a decision has been made, or after the action has been started or completed. Justification is then the only way of achieving consistency, be it by explaining and defending the action before or after the decision, or before or after the action. If the constituency has no very complex ideas on certain difficult issues, the executives and representatives can act towards it in the role of transmitters. The constituency will often be easier to convince than the actors.

Justification means that consistency is preferred to control, but it does not necessarily mean that the lack of control becomes evident. As argued above, if the ideas of the executive are created in a complex process of interaction and discussion with the actors, it may be very difficult to work out who is controlling whom. Rather, the formal hierarchy of constituency, executive, and actors may be enough to create the illusion that the first are controlling the last. If decisions are made before action is taken, this impression will be reinforced. Paradoxically, forceful justification on the part of the executives can give the impression that they are in fact in strong control. Since they are obviously so convinced about what action is the right one, there seems no reason to believe that they have not controlled it.

If executives are successful in convincing others of their controlling role, they become responsible for the decision and for the action: in our culture responsibility is the effect of perceived control (Edwards 1959; Ross 1975; Aristotle 1984: Book 3). They become 'leaders'. Through their responsibility the executives are bound to the action. This makes it even more important for them to defend the decision and the action; they are also defending themselves.

Thus executives who put great effort into seeking control may easily reveal their failure to achieve either control or consistency. Those who go in for justification have a better chance of appearing successful as regards both consistency and control. The effects are similar for representatives behaving in the same way.

Furthermore, justification can sometimes be combined with some degree of influence over actions. The executives may be able to choose whether or not to justify some of the actors' actions by making or not making decisions about them. Actions lacking decisions may be delayed or stopped altogether, since they are not supported by the legitimacy attaching to the executives. Similarly the representatives may refuse making decisions or the constituency may refuse to accept certain actions. This right to refrain from decision or acceptance can offer an alternative conception of the way the constituency–actor model works, an alternative to the model which we have discussed above, whereby ideas control actions by preceding and steering them. In order to exert this right it appears that accounting and evaluation and the election of representatives and executives based on their earlier achievements, are all more useful than budgets, plans, or promises about future achievements.

Executives and representatives who see their role as one of reacting to rather than controlling actions by steering them, may appear less influential and therefore become less responsible. Nor do they need to keep in close contact with the actors. Both these factors make it easier for them to reject proposed actions, to say no (Jacobsson 1984, 1989; Brunsson 1989). So, more modest ambitions regarding control may well mean more influence.

Justification can solve the problem of the lack of consistency which stems from differences in the original ideas of the constituency and those of the actors. It can also prevent the lack of consistency that arises because ideas change more quickly than action. Since justification means that ideas are adapted to action, for it to succeed it is necessary that the ideas are flexible—just as the adaptation of action to ideas requires flexible actions. The more ideas surpass actions in flexibility, the more justification is likely to achieve.

But justification cannot solve the problem of inconsistency when it arises from differences in what can be said and what can be done. Actions that cannot be stated cannot be defended. In order to solve that problem, we have to accept hypocrisy.

Hypocrisy

Justification means that representatives, executives, or actors produce and present ideas. But when presenting ideas their repertoire is not necessarily limited to justification, that is, to expressing ideas in accordance with planned or accomplished actions. They can also produce ideas that are inconsistent with actions, that is, they can produce hypocrisy. Actions that are difficult to justify can be compensated for by talk in the opposite direction. Decisions, too, can be part of hypocrisy; they can be contrary to actions, compensating for action rather than controlling or justifying it. Through hypocrisy, the ideas of the constituency are isolated from action. But the constituency's ideas can control the ideas presented by representatives, executives, and actors: there is no incentive to express opinions other than those displayed by the constituency.

Hypocrisy may provide the only chance of achieving some action without the risk of losing general support for the representatives, executives, or actors, and thus also for the action. Satisfying one opinion by way of talk, decision, and action may bring support from a few extremists only, from the true believers in a single idea. For instance, when public opinion is divided between socialists and liberals it may be easier for socialist governments than for liberal governments to carry out liberal political action, and vice versa. It may be necessary to compensate for socialist action by liberal talk, as well as the other way round. In this way both liberals and socialists may be relatively satisfied.

If hypocrisy is to facilitate action without undermining the general support for decision-makers and actors, then the constituency must deem important not only what actions are taken but also what decisions and talk are produced. There can be two main reasons for this. One is that people regard talk and decisions as important in themselves. After all, the contact between representatives and executives on the one hand and actions on the other is often uncertain and ambiguous, while people can feel much more certain about talk and decisions; it is easier to know that representatives and executives say what they say and decide what they decide than to know that their talk and decisions affect action in any specific way. And if their role is just to talk and decide, it seems reasonable to consider it important that they express good ideas and decisions rather than bad ones. The representatives and executives are appreciated for their good intentions and ideas, while energy and results are criteria for evaluating actors. This may be particularly relevant in the case of large organizations or political bodies. The more remote representatives and executives are from the action and the less influence they have upon it, the more reason there is to consider their talk and decisions as important in themselves.

A second reason is the opposite of the first one, namely that talk and decisions are seen as lacking any intrinsic value but are valuable only because they are supposed to lead to action. Just because the ultimate goal is action, talk and decisions acquire a related value. The more strongly it is believed that representative or executive talk and decisions do control action, the greater the relevance of the talk and decisions. Representatives and executives often reinforce such interpretations, perhaps by formulating their talk and decisions as goals and visions for the future. Today's action can then be excused by reference to the future. The only chance of getting pollution accepted today may be to claim that the goal or plan is to reduce or stop it in the future.

Hypocrisy has several advantages over justification. First, it is a way of handling the problem of the difference between what can be said and what can be done. Hypocrisy means that what can and should be said is said, not only by ordinary people but also by important people such as representatives or executives, but without the talk leading to the corresponding action. What can be said is said, what can be done is done. Second, control is exerted in the right direction. Unlike the case of justification, important talk and decisions can be controlled by the ideas of the constituency, not the other way round. Third, a certain consistency is achieved, albeit not between ideas and action but between ideas and talk and decisions. Fourth, hypocrisy seems to occupy a higher moral position than justification: instead of some people defending bad actions, everyone is arguing for the right ideas (March 1978). This is particularly important when the difference between what can be said and what can be done is determined by ethical norms.

Unlike both control and justification, hypocrisy can reflect opinions that are severely divided (Brunsson 1989). Different opinions can be reflected in talk, decisions, and actions, allowing for the reflection of at least three different views in all. Furthermore, since talk and decisions are not related to action, it is easier to accept variations and contradictions in talk and decisions. Thus a broad spectrum of opinion can be reflected.

Justification can only succeed if the ideas of the constituency can in fact be influenced. If people hold strong and stable opinions which cannot be converted into action, then hypocrisy provides the only chance of effecting some control and consistency. Despite attempts at justification, opinions can remain divided; they may even become more divided (Nisbett and Ross 1980: ch. 8). In such cases hypocrisy could lead to greater consistency than either control or justification.

Neither justification nor hypocrisy necessarily require much if any energy or mobilization. Whether or not they wish it, actors, representatives, and executives often find themselves compelled to defend actions that they may not even approve of any more, but which cannot be changed, perhaps for economic or contractual reasons or on grounds of credibility. Hypocrisy can be the result of the decision-makers' failure to control action, with a resulting discrepancy between decision and action. Discrepancies between talk and contradictory talk and decisions are all natural results of the activities of assemblies such as parliaments and councils, in which a variety of ideas are represented and majorities are continually shifting.

THE PRACTICAL EFFECTS OF IMPRACTICAL MODELS

This chapter has indicated a number of difficulties in achieving consistency between ideas and actions and getting ideas to control actions in a constituency–actor structure. Ideas do not always control actions; I have indicated three other relationships between ideas and action. One posits a lack of connection: ideas and action are not related at all; they constitute two worlds without influence on each other. Another implies that action controls ideas. A third relationship implies that ideas and action are systematically inconsistent, that the expression of ideas pointing in one direction facilitates action in the opposite direction. Even if ideas control actions the two are not necessarily consistent. Consistency may sometimes be achieved by letting action control ideas; or talk and decisions can be controlled by—and consistent with—ideas, without actions being either controlled by or consistent with ideas.

I have also noted a number of conditions that cause problems for control and consistency. In conclusion I will now look at some conditions under which consistency and control could be achieved more easily in the constituency–actor model. Let us first consider what ideas are acceptable according to these criteria.

One requirement is that action alone has any intrinsic value. Ideas are about action, and people are interested in the action and not in the ideas for their own sake. Expressions such as 'talk' and 'symbols' carry a negative charge. This materialistic orientation can prevent the acceptance of hypocrisy, but does not necessarily do so. Even materialists may regard talk as important if they believe it to be a step towards action. So it is important that they should not be mistaken, something which can be ensured by the second and third requirements presented below.

The second requirement is that it is possible to do what is said and vice versa. Control and consistency are not easy to attain when ideas evolve without any connection with the way actions develop. This means that frankness and realism are important; there should be no taboos; it should be possible to discuss everything openly, and opinions should not be too wild but should keep within the realm of the possible. This calls for enlightened constituencies with good knowledge of what is feasible. Ideas must also be clear and coherent, so that there is no ambiguity about which actions are consistent with them and which are not. Such clarity can be achieved in two completely different ways. Either the actions are clearly specified in great detail and there is control over the details; or the amount of control that is aimed for is more modest, with the constituency or its representatives perhaps formulating general goals and the executives or actors being free to choose the means for attaining them.

A third requirement is that the ideas change more slowly than the action is implemented. Also, the action should not influence the ideas. Thus stable ideas are better than unstable ones. Decisions can stabilize ideas. Or a stabilizing effect can be achieved if stable ideas are the only ones to be expressed. Basic goals and values are often assumed to be more stable than ideas about details. This kind of assumption leads to the claim that the relevant sphere of ideas for the constituency concerns basic values and goals, while details should be left to the actors.

Finally, a fourth requirement is that the ideas of the principals in the constituency–actor structure should not be influenced by the opinions of the agents. This can be achieved by letting contact proceed in one direction only, thus preserving the notion of the strict hierarchy of constituency, representatives, executives, and actors. The problem can also be solved by assuming that agents such as actors present not opinions but only 'facts', if it is believed that mere facts do not influence fundamental values and their role is supposed to be to provide a good basis for 'realistic' opinions.

All these conditions under which ideas can control action are elements in traditional and popular conceptions of the rational individual: human beings hold stable preferences which control but are not controlled by their actions; it is possible to distinguish between preferences and facts or consequences; preferences have no value of their own, and there are no actions that are not controlled by preferences. Ideas control action.

Claims that ideas should be of this kind are also part of much of the traditional wisdom of administration. Concepts such as action orientation, frankness, realism, clear decisions, commitment to decisions, clear goals, respect for facts, and management by objectives are all positive terms, while symbol politics, lack of openness, unrealism, lack of clarity in goals or between values and facts, long decision processes, inadequate commitment to decisions, and decision-makers' intervention at the level of detail all have a more negative ring. The positive terms make it sound more likely that ideas can control and be consistent with action.

Thus the norms of control and consistency seem to generate norms about the acceptable nature of ideas. This contradicts the notion that the constituency's ideas (whatever they are) should provide the basis for action, for instance that the opinions of the electorate should constitute the basic independent variable in democracy, or the opinions of the owners should steer company action. In this context we would instead expect norms requiring the adaptation of action to any form of ideas, be they rational or irrational. Acceptable actions would be the quick ones with no long-term effects, and the simple ones requiring little knowledge.

But rational assumptions are seldom very realistic. Instead the relationship between ideas and action can often be expected to be one of isolation, justification, or hypocrisy—all of which can appear even if many representatives and executives are actually striving for control and consistency. Furthermore, people in these positions may sometimes avoid seeking control since such behaviour can actually bring them less influence than a strategy of justification.

Presentation and Result

What has been said above does not mean that the way in which relations between ideas and action are presented is not important. The mode of presentation may have great practical effects. As was mentioned in the introduction above, organizations and societies are often presented as creating consistency between ideas and action by control; the constituency is controlling the representatives who control the executives who control the actors. The representatives or executives make decisions, and these decisions are perceived as their choice of certain actions and as a means of controlling what actions are taken. Even if this kind of presentation seldom provides a very realistic description of what happens in practice, it may still have considerable practical effects. At least if it is believed, it creates and attributes responsibility. The decision-makers are presented as influential and consequently responsible people.

If specific people are responsible, then we know who to blame or praise. If executives or representatives are held responsible, it seems sensible to replace them when actions turn out to be wrong; and if the constituency itself is ultimately responsible, there is not much to be done; the situation is a legitimate and stable one. Moreover, actions gain legitimacy if the representatives, or the constituency itself, are responsible for them, and this makes it easier to carry them out. The presentation of consistency and control creates legitimacy and the power to act—two fundamental qualities of modern organizations and societies.

One conclusion is thus that the individual model with its emphasis on consistency and control is in itself an example of something that can be said but can seldom be done. It is closely associated with important normative ideas in our society about the individual and rationality; it constitutes an example of a broadly shared and stable idea and value. It is easy to talk about, while its presentation also has major beneficial effects. The model of consistency and control ought to be talked about. But it can be put into effect in practice to a limited extent only. The other relations between ideas and action can be effected to a greater extent, but they cannot be talked about without having awkward effects on our conceptions of ourselves, on the attribution of responsibility, and consequently on legitimacy and the power to act. To defend the model of control and consistency is therefore a crucial task for those who influence ideas and mould opinion. Its defence by representatives or executives often involves hypocrisy—a type of hypocrisy which safeguards the good ideas but which is in itself an example of the fact that it may be difficult or inappropriate to achieve good ideas in practice.

REFERENCES

Aristotle (1984). *The Nicomanchean Ethics*. Oxford: Oxford University Press.

Baier, V. E., March, J. G., and Saetren, H. (1986). 'Implementation and Ambiguity', *Scandinavian Journal of Management Studies*, 2(3–4): 197–212.

Berger, P. and Luckmann, T. (1966). *The Social Construction of Reality*. Garden City, NY: Doubleday.

Brunsson, N. (1985). *The Irrational Organization. Irrationality as a Basis for Organizational Action and Change*. Chichester, UK: Wiley.

——(1989). *The Organization of Hyprocrisy. Talk, Decisions and Actions in Organizations*. Chichester, UK: Wiley.

——and Jönsson, S. A. (1979). *Beslut och handling*. Stockholm: Liber.

——and Olsen, J. P. (1993). *The Reforming Organization*. London: Routledge.

Cohen, M., March, J. G., and Olsen, J. P. (1972). 'A Garbage Can Model of Rational Choice', *Administrative Science Quarterly*, 17: 1–25.

Cyert, R. M. and March, J. G. (1963). *A Behavioral Theory of the Firm*. Englewood Cliffs, NJ: Prentice-Hall.

Edwards, R. B. (1959). *Freedom, Responsibility and Obligation*. The Hague: Martinus Nijhoff.

Forssell, A. (1989). 'How to Become Modern and Businesslike: An Attempt to Understand the Modernization of Swedish Savings Banks', *International Studies of Management & Organization*, 19(3): 34–48.

Granovetter, M. (1985). 'Economic Action and Social Structure: The Problems of Embeddedness', *American Journal of Sociology*, 91(3): 481–510.

Hanf, K. and Scharpf, F. W. (eds.) (1978). *Interorganizational Policy Making*. London: Sage.

Hägg, I. and Johanson, J. (eds.) (1982). *Företag i nätvek-ny syn på konkurrenskraft*. Stockholm: SNS.

Håkansson, H. (1989). *Corporate Technological Behaviour. Co-operation and Networks*. London: Routledge.

Harmon, M. M. (1989). ' "Decision" and "Action" as Contrasting Perspectives in Organization Theory', *Public Administration Review*, 49(2): 144–50.

Hirdman, Y. (1989). *Att lägga livet tillrätta*. Stockholm: Carlssons.

Jacobsson, B. (1984). *Hur styrs förvaltningen?* Lund: Studentlitteratur.

_____ (1989). *Konsten att reagera*. Stockholm: Carlssons.

Kingdon, J. (1984). *Agendas. Alternatives and Public Policies*. Boston, MA: Little Brown.

March, J. G. (1978). 'Bounded Rationality, Ambiguity and the Engineering of Choice', *Bell Journal of Economics*, 9(2): 587–608.

_____ and Olsen, J. P. (1976). *Ambiguity and Choice in Organizations*. Bergen: Universitetsforlaget.

_____ _____ (1989). *Rediscovering Institutions*. New York: Free Press.

Mandeville, B. ([1724] 1966). *The Fable of the Bees or Private Vices, Public Benefits*. Oxford: Oxford University Press.

Meyer, J., Boli, J., and Thomas, G. (1987). 'Ontology and Rationalization in the Western Cultural Account', in G. Thomas, J. Meyer, F. Ramorcz, and J. Boli (eds.), *Institutional Structure*. Beverly Hills, CA: Sage.

_____ and Rowan, B. (1977). 'Institutionalized Organizations: Formal Structure as Myth and Ceremony', *American Journal of Sociology*, 83(2): 340–63.

Nisbett, R. and Ross, L. (1980). *Human Inference*. Englewood Cliffs, NJ: Prentice-Hall.

Olsen, J. P. (ed.) (1991). *Svensk demokrati i förändring*. Stockholm: Carlssons.

Pressman, J. and Wildavsky, A. (1973). *Implementation*. Berkeley, CA: University of California Press.

Ross, A. (1975). *On Guilt Responsibility and Punishment*. London: Stevens.

Sandelands, L. E. (1990). 'What Is so Practical About Theory? Lewin Revisited', *Journal for the Theory of Social Behaviour*, 20(3): 235–62.

Scott, R. W. (1992). *Organizations. Rational, Natural and Open Systems*, 3rd edn. Englewood Cliffs, NJ: Prentice-Hall.

Segal, J. (1990). Alternative Conceptions of the Economic Realm. Paper presented at the second Conference on Socio-Economics, Washington.

Selznick, P. ([1949]1965). *TVA and the Grass-Roots*. New York: Harper & Row.

Wildavsky, A. (1974). *The Politics of the Budgetary Process*. Boston, MA: Little Brown.

Zajonc, R. (1960). 'The Process of Cognitive Tuning in Communication', *Journal of Abnormal and Social Psychology*, 61: 159–67.

Index